SCIENCE STUDY SKILLS PROGRAM:

People, Energy, and Appropriate Technology

Developed by The Study Skills Group

Authors: Carol Wilson
Science Department
Dr. Mark T. Sheehan High School
Wallingford, Connecticut

Gary Krasnow, *Director*
Renewable Energy Resource Center
Connecticut Audubon Society

Editor: Lisa Smulyan
Bureau of Study Counsel
Harvard University

Senior Editor: David Marshak

Editorial Board: Kiyo Morimoto, *Director*
Bureau of Study Counsel
Harvard University

Jerome Pieh, *Headmaster*
Milton Academy

James J. McGuinn

NSTA

National Science Teachers Association
Washington, DC 20009

The National Association of Secondary School Principals
Reston, Virginia 22091

Graph on pages 47 and 48 of the Student Text adapted from *Environmental Trends.* Washington, D.C.: Council on Environmental Quality, Executive Office of the President, 1981. Page 182.

Illustrator: Linda Sokol

ISBN 0-88210-151-X

TABLE OF CONTENTS

INTRODUCTION

Study skills in science are essential for effective learning. They include a wide array of methods which facilitate good academic performance and help students make more efficient use of class and study time.

Science has its own vocabulary, notation, and procedures. Just as working with scientific measuring tools is a learned skill, so are problem solving and "taking command of a test." We need to take the responsibility for teaching science study skills because they are critical to our students' success in learning in the science classroom.

Many students who are doing well in science can develop more efficient study skills. They can also benefit from learning how to organize their skills into a useful system. Others who are doing poorly may lack proficiency in study skills and will need to learn both the skills and systematic ways of using them. Many of these students think they do not have the necessary ability, but the problem is often the combination of a lack of study skills and a minimum of self confidence. When these students learn effective study skills, they become more competent and more confident learners.

Study Skills in Science: What Are They?

Study skills are procedures for acquiring knowledge and competence. In science they include such skills as interpreting charts and graphs, using scientific measuring tools, working in scientific notation, and developing and testing hypotheses. Study skills such as listening, building vocabulary, taking effective notes, and reading for meaning are other skills which are basic to all learning and of value to students in the science classroom.

In a larger sense, science study skills are strategies and methods for solving problems of any sort. The student who gains mastery of science study skills is really discovering how to learn effectively in any situation.

Study Skills and Independent Learning

When students develop a repertoire of study skills, they become more independent as learners. For example, many students who can follow a set of directions when the teacher is present may experience great difficulty when they must work on their own, either in school or at home. Students who know how to follow directions, use resources, develop a study plan, and analyze problems will be more successful as independent learners.

Students learn study skills best when they have the opportunity to try a variety of study or learning strategies, decide which ones are most effective for them, and gradually refine those strategies into an effective study system.

Science Study Skills and Basic Skills

In a position statement adopted in 1982, the National Science Teachers Association (NSTA) described the goal of science education as developing scientifically literate individuals who understand how science, technology, and society influence one another and who are able to use this knowledge in their everyday decision making. The **hm Science Study Skills Program** is based in part on the NSTA's statement that the scientifically and technologically literate person:

- uses science concepts, process skills, and values in making responsible everyday decisions;

- understands how society influences science and technology as well as how science and technology influence society;

- understands that society controls science and technology through the allocation of resources;

- recognizes the limitations as well as the usefulness of science and technology in advancing human welfare;

- distinguishes between scientific evidence and personal opinion; and

- understands the applications of technology and the decisions involved in the use of technology.

THE hm SCIENCE STUDY SKILLS PROGRAM

The **hm Science Study Skills Program** is designed to provide an introduction to study skills in science for students in grades 7–10 through a series of 14 activity-oriented units. Some of the units will require one period of class time. Others will require two periods or more.

The units progress from basic skills such as listening and reading for meaning to more complex skills like problem solving, working in scientific notation, and developing and testing an hypothesis. The program culminates in a class project which permits students to use many of the science study skills they have learned.

FOCUS ON PEOPLE, ENERGY, AND TECHNOLOGY

Unlike the other books in the hm series which focus strictly on study skills, this program also provides instruction in a specific content area within the 7th–10th grade general science curriculum. The same activities which enable students to practice science study skills also introduce them to a variety of technologies for collecting, transferring, storing, and conserving energy. In addition, students can begin to discover how the decisions made about energy today affect the technologies they will rely on for food, shelter, and transportation in the decades to come.

Appropriate Technology

While people, energy, and technology are the subjects of the **hm Science Study Skills Program**, "appropriateness" is the unifying theme. Unit I poses the question, "What Does Appropriate Mean?" The next six units apply the concept of appropriateness to technology:

- Unit II illustrates why technologies which use locally available resources are preferable to those which import them from far away.

- Units III and IV explain why technologies which use renewable sources of energy are preferable to those which rely on finite sources, such as coal, oil, and natural gas.

- Unit V stresses the importance of minimizing the environmental impact of technology.

- Unit VI stresses the importance of minimizing technological waste and inefficiency.

- Unit VII demonstrates the usefulness of life cycle cost analysis when choosing among competing technologies.

These first seven units serve to establish a set of criteria which students can use to assess the appropriateness of any technology. Unit VIII tests students' understanding of these ideas.

The Solar Greenhouse

In the second section of the book (Units IX–XII), students take a closer look at one example of appropriate technology: the attached solar greenhouse which can be used to produce food and heat. The solar greenhouse is a small-scale, simple structure which embodies in microcosm all of the characteristics of appropriate technology presented in the first seven units:

- it relies primarily on passive solar energy, a locally available, renewable resource;
- it has minimal impact on the environment;
- when properly designed and constructed, it is extremely efficient in its use of energy; and
- it withstands the test of life-cycle cost analysis.

In Unit IX, students experiment to discover how a solar greenhouse traps and retains the sun's energy. Unit X introduces students to the scientific laws which explain how energy behaves in a solar greenhouse. In Unit XI, students again experiment, this time with ways of storing solar energy. In Unit XII they work with ways of conserving energy in a solar greenhouse and the structure to which it is attached.

Appropriate Technology in Action

The third and final section of the book gives students an opportunity to apply what they have learned about appropriate technology. In Unit XIII, students design and test either a wind machine or a passive solar collector. In Unit XIV, they design and implement an appropriate technology aimed at solving a problem within their own school. The science study skills presented in the first 13 units will be useful to students as they work on this project.

SCIENCE STUDY SKILLS AND LEARNING BY DOING

The **hm Science Study Skills Program** is based on the assumption that activity-oriented lessons are the most effective way to teach study skills; more succinctly, that "learning by doing" is the best way to master study skills. In the activities in the **hm Program,** students will both learn about study skills needed for science and practice these skills in a science environment.

The program is deliberately designed to meet a wide range of student needs:

1. For the student who has little sense of a particular study skill, it provides an introduction to that skill.
2. For the student who is ready to acquire a skill, it provides an initial learning experience.
3. For the student who has mastered a skill, participation offers review and reinforcement.

Thus, the **Program's** exercises allow for the participation of students with a diversity of skills and promote learning on various levels of competence.

USING THE hm SCIENCE STUDY SKILLS PROGRAM: WHERE AND WHEN

We suggest that the **hm Science Study Skills Program** be taught as one unit of an ongoing general science course. Only in the regular science classroom can the teacher of the **hm Program** show the student the immediate and long-term value of mastering the various skills.

Our classroom testing has shown the applicability of the **hm Program** in grades 7–10. It may also be of value to students at other grade levels.

Our testing clearly demonstrated that teachers found the program most successful when they used the units in sequence from beginning to end. Some teachers found it possible to use the first eight units at one time and the last six at another time or to use individual units in conjunction with other, ongoing science curricula. We suggest that you discover the most beneficial way of integrating the **Program** into your curriculum through your own experience with its use.

SUGGESTIONS FOR TEACHING
THE hm SCIENCE STUDY SKILLS PROGRAM

Background for the Teacher

Each unit in the Teacher's Guide begins with background information for the teacher about both the study skills to be presented and whatever facet of energy or appropriate technology is covered in the unit. In most cases, the information about energy and technology goes beyond the material presented to the student so that you can be in a position to field questions with greater confidence. In some cases, additional background information is presented in an appendix. The teacher who wishes to become even more familiar with the material will find numerous sources of additional information in the selective bibliography at the end of the Teacher's Guide.

Suggested Directions

1. The Teacher's Guide offers "Suggested Directions" for teaching each unit in the **Program**. Our classroom testing has shown these methods to be useful. Of course, we invite you to adapt them in ways which you see fit.

2. We suggest that you examine both the Student Text and the Teacher's Guide carefully prior to your teaching of the various units. *All of the material in the Student Text has been included in the Teacher's Guide.* Answers to student exercises have been added to the Student Text pages in the Teacher's Guide where appropriate.

Suggested Times

1. The units in this **Program** are structured to accommodate the teacher who meets with his or her class for one period in a given day.

2. Each section of the "Suggested Directions" in the Teacher's Guide includes approximate times for the various parts of the units. We caution you that these times are approximate.

Our classroom testing experience has shown us that the wide variation in teacher style results in an equally wide range in the pacing of instruction. We strongly suggest that you examine the **Program** units carefully and gauge your planning of instructional time according to your knowledge of how things actually work in your classroom.

Unit Summaries

1. Each unit concludes with a summary. Since Unit VIII ("Becoming a Skilled Test Taker and Appropriate Technology in Review") advises students to review these unit summaries in preparation for an upcoming test, we strongly recommend that you bring them to the attention of your students at the end of each unit.

Additional Suggestions and Information

1. Students will need additional activities beyond the scope of this **Program** to practice and reinforce their acquisition of science study skills. Some ideas for the extension of the various units are included with each section of this Teacher's Guide and are entitled "Additional Suggestions."

2. You will find a selective bibliography and several technical appendices about energy and appropriate technology following Unit XIV. A glossary of energy terms is included at the end of both the Teacher's Guide and the Student Text.

Advance Preparation

1. Many of the units in the **hm Science Study Skills Program** require you to duplicate information for students or to provide them with materials for their experiments. A complete list of these units and what they require is given on the next page. We suggest that you try out the experiments and work through all of the mathematical calculations in each unit before assigning them to your students.

UNITS WHICH REQUIRE ADVANCE PREPARATION OR MATERIALS

UNIT	EXERCISE	PREPARATION
I	II	Duplicate copies of passages A, B, and C.
III and IV		You may want to update numbers used in passages in these units. See Unit III for references.
V	III	Duplicate copies of information on houses.
VIII		Duplicate copies of Unit I–VII Review Test. You may also need copies of another test with which students can practice test taking skills.
IX	I	Thermometers needed.
	II	Protractors needed.
	III	*Materials for experiment:* protractors / cardboard / glass jars with screw-on lids / watch or clock / light source
	IV	*Materials for experiment:* same as above plus insulating materials such as construction paper, cloth, wool.
X	II	*Materials for experiment:* beaker and ring stand / Bunsen burner / sawdust
	III	*Materials for experiment:* light bulbs / cardboard
XI	II	*Materials for experiment:* glass jars with screw-on lids / Celsius thermometers / energy source (heat lamp or sun) / storage materials (sand, rocks, water, wood chips, clay)
XIII	II and IV	*Materials for testing solar collectors and wind machines:* energy source (sun or heat lamp) / thermometers / string / weights

TEACHING THE hm SCIENCE STUDY SKILLS PROGRAM: A POTPOURRI OF HINTS AND SUGGESTIONS

Small Groups

Most of the units in the **hm Science Study Skills Program** are suitable for whole class or small group instruction. We highly recommend that you give your students the opportunity to work in groups of two, three, or four. If students work with a partner, we suggest that you pair students of generally similar ability.

The interaction of students working on a common task can facilitate the learning of skills through shared problem solving. In this way students can learn from each other.

Small group processes offer a useful method for genuinely engaging students in an activity. Such processes help both to enhance motivation for learning and to increase interest in the content of the lesson, as they offer active participation to each and every student.

Individual Work in Study Skills

Individual work is of critical importance to the learning of skills. When a skill is introduced in a group setting, it becomes crucial to provide individual work with that skill through homework and/or other class activities.

Student Discussion and Learning

To learn study skills effectively and know how and when to use them, students need the opportunity to discuss their work. Their discussion must include not only the "right answer" but the process through which they arrived at the answer and their reasons for considering it correct. At this point in your students' development of study skills, the process is more important than the individual answer.

Using Calculators

Students will find calculators helpful in Units XI and XII. One calculator for every two or three students is enough. If calculators are not available in the school, students may be able to bring them from home. The use of calculators will not detract from students' activities in these units but will help them see calculators as useful scientific tools.

Student Perceptions and Expectations

Sometimes students perceive new study skills as more time-consuming than their unskilled learning behaviors. In a few cases, this is an accurate perception, but most often it is not.

You can help students gain a wider perspective about their own learning by telling them that any skill, by its very nature, takes more time to use when you are first learning how to do it. Then, as you become more competent in using the skill, it takes less and less time. Ask students to think of examples of this from their own experience. Or, give them a few examples which will illustrate this relationship between competence and time.

Grading

Given the grade-oriented reality of most classrooms, we suggest that the student's involvement with the **hm Program** be evaluated in some fair and concrete manner. Your standard of evaluation ought to keep in mind the process of how skills are learned, namely through repeated practice over time, and set reasonable levels of expected mastery. We also suggest that you inform your students about how their work with the **hm Program** will be evaluated at the very beginning of their use of the **Program**.

Unit VIII includes a test of students' understanding of the information on energy and technology presented in Units I–VII. As explained in the Teacher's Guide to that unit, the test may be given as a test or can be used in the unit's exercises which help students practice test taking skills. The projects students design and implement in Unit XIV can also be used to evaluate their understanding of the scientific principles taught in the **Program**.

An Overview of Study Skills

During the past decade, many educators have defined basic skills primarily in terms of communication and computation skills. Study skills, though often neglected or ignored, are also basic skills. These skills for learning are at the core of educative process.

WHAT ARE STUDY SKILLS?

Study skills are learned abilities for acquiring knowledge or competence. The table of contents of a study skills handbook or text usually includes, among others, the following skill areas: listening, textbook reading, note taking, planning your time, study behavior and environment, vocabulary skills, and test taking. These skills and others which fit into the category of study skills directly relate to many of the activities in which students are engaged while they are in school or doing schoolwork.

A broader definition of study skills or learning skills views them as processes for learning. When one learns a study skill, one is learning more than a specific technique. One is learning a way of problem solving, a method which can be used in any relevant context. One is also learning more about how to learn effectively and how to be in charge of one's own learning. It is this perception of study skills as transferable processes for learning which reveals the critical importance of these skills.

A review of nearly 80 years of study skills literature indicates that, at least throughout this century, the nature of study skills has remained relatively constant. Study skills in 1940 were much like those in 1920, in 1960, and even in 1980. There have been variations of emphasis as well as some genuinely innovative developments over the years, but the strongest impression is one of continuity.

This continuity is important to keep in mind in view of the trendy nature of American education which often seems to produce a good deal of ill-considered change. Even though an element of the curriculum is found to be useful, we still often choose to eliminate or ignore it whenever the next new trend appears. Because study skills have been relatively impervious to change, they have been periodically discarded over the years, only to be rediscovered much later. This pendulum effect has had damaging results because the importance of learning how to learn never diminishes.

HOW HAVE STUDY SKILLS BEEN TAUGHT?

The most common approach to study skills instruction during the first few decades of this century was essentially the preaching of morality. This approach related good study skills to what was called "high morals," indicating that students who displayed the correct moral values would be the ones with good study skills.

This moralistic approach to the teaching of study skills peaked before World War II, at least if the literature is an accurate guide, and was replaced by a focus on techniques and formulae. The most famous of these formulaic methods is SQ3R, an excellent method for reading a textbook which was developed by F. P. Robinson.

The chief characteristic of a formulaic approach to study skills is the learning of a specific series of behaviors. For example, using SQ3R, one learns to survey, question, read, recite, and review. Unfortunately the use of such formulae often descends to the level of gimmickry. Students are taught to use a particular technique as if it involved an act of magic; that is, something beyond their active and conscious participation, comprehension, and control. Although formulaic methods attempt to create understanding and involvement in the student, the mere fact of their use guarantees neither of these necessary outcomes.

While formulaic techniques can be very useful, they must be employed within a framework for the teaching of study skills which engages the student not only in learning a particular skill but also in learning about what happens within oneself when one learns and uses a study skill. It is important for the student to learn why a skill works and why it is valuable as he or she is learning how to do it. A central part of this learning involves the student's initiative in the exercise of judgment and choice.

A third method of teaching study skills is the handbook approach. While this method claims to understand and appreciate the value of study skills, it argues that no class time is available for study skills instruction. Thus, this approach relies on the handbook to elicit involvement and learning. Students are given written descriptions of various study skills and are expected somehow to translate verbal abstractions into behavior. A few students can and will make this leap, but the vast majority cannot, because they lack the motivation, self-discipline, and conceptual ability required to learn study skills independently. Though not uncommon, the handbook approach is not particularly helpful. Although it is an effort to address the need for teaching study skills, its use results in a minimum of learning while simultaneously creating frustration and resistance in the student.

STATUS OF STUDY SKILLS TEACHING

The overview of study skills instruction presented below is primarily drawn from two sources: the editors' observations throughout the country over the past 11 years, and a national survey conducted by one of their colleagues. While this overview is a generalization to which specific contradictions can certainly be cited, the larger picture which it offers seems accurate.

During the past several years, the "back to basics" movement has led to a greater emphasis on basic skills during the middle school/junior high years. However, this movement has not addressed the lack of effective study skills instruction in most middle/junior high and high school curricula. Despite the renewed concern for skills education, the widespread failure to regard study skills as basic skills has resulted in a continuing lack of emphasis on study skills instruction.

Another problem involves the nature of study skills teaching which does take place. Though many teachers do include some study skills instruction in their curricula, they tend to do so with a lack of focus on precisely what skills they wish to teach and on how their students' learning is going to occur. This absence of focus results in a lack of coordination of their efforts toward the teaching of study skills in any given class over the course of the year. Rather than a well-planned, highly coordinated effort, what often results is the haphazard collection of insufficiently related lessons.

A third shortcoming is the lack of coordination of efforts in teaching study skills among teachers of different subjects at the same grade level. While there is some uncertainty and conflict in regard to the responsibility for teaching other basic skills, this confusion is particularly intense in regard to study skills. For example, is the English teacher the only one who is responsible for teaching the various communication skills which are also study skills? Or should every teacher deal with these in some way relevant to his or her own subject? The reality is that schools often fail to delineate the areas of responsibility for the teaching of study skills. It is no wonder that confusion arises among teachers; ultimately, though, it is the students who suffer most.

A fourth problem is an extension of the previous one: not only do schools fail to coordinate and organize the teaching of study skills in any particular grade, but the same phenomenon also takes place on a system-wide basis throughout a student's academic career. Teachers often assume that somebody else has taught certain skills to their students or will teach them later on. But often no one ever gets around to teaching them because there is no clear assignment of responsibility.

HOW DO WE TEACH STUDY SKILLS?

People learn skills through processes of repeated trial and error. One key to effective study skills teaching, then, is providing the student with sufficient opportunity for practice of the skills to be learned. Of course, there is an inevitable tension between providing students with trial and error practice of a new study skill and helping students to maintain their interest in learning the skill in the face of the necessary repetition. While this tension cannot be removed, it can be minimized by acknowledging the tension as a natural part of learning something new, and through the use of varied and imaginative instructional design.

A second key to study skills teaching is the recognition that learning a study skill requires the learner to err before he or she can succeed. We learn skills by trying to use a new skill, making mistakes, identifying our mistakes and learning from them, and then correcting our mistakes. This understanding creates several responsibilities for the teacher:

1. The teacher provides a space within the learning process where the student can try out a new skill, experience a good deal of error, but not feel that he or she has failed or is a failure.

2. The teacher provides usable feedback to the student about the effectiveness of the student's use of the new study skill.

3. The teacher rewards the student for what he or she has done well in using the new study skill. With such recognition, the student experiences success in the learning process and will be more motivated to continue the development of mastery in the new study skill. Recognition involves the acknowledgement of the effort to risk in the face of possible failure.

In addition to these two key understandings, a program of effective study skills instruction would be based on the following underlying values:

1. Study skills need to be defined as processes for learning.

2. Study skills need to be included within the cluster of basic skills.

3. An important part of learning study skills involves learning more about how one learns. Thus, instruction in study skills engages the student in an active participation in his or her own learning. The student is encouraged and provided with the opportunity to develop the ability to exercise his or her own judgment in regard to the learning and use of study skills.

4. Learning by doing is the best way to learn study skills.

5. A considerable part of study skills instruction ought to take place during class time. Such instruction should also be integrated with the regular curriculum of the course.

6. The learning of study skills offers a transfer effect; a skill learned in relation to one subject can be applied to any other relevant context.

7. The work of various developmental psychologists has shown us that there is a continuum of cognitive development throughout the years of childhood and adolescence, and that people are only able to deal successfully with learning tasks which are appropriate for their level of development. It is crucial to relate this insight to the teaching of study skills and to ask a student to learn only what is within the realm of his or her cognitive ability at that level of development.

PART ONE:

WHAT MAKES A TECHNOLOGY APPROPRIATE?

UNIT I: LISTENING AS A SCIENCE SKILL
and
WHAT DOES APPROPRIATE MEAN?

STUDY SKILLS

Listening means more than just hearing. Listening means hearing *and* understanding.

This unit is designed to introduce the student to the idea of listening as a set of skills which can be learned. Its activities present several specific listening skills to the student and give her or him the opportunity to learn how to use these skills.

The unit also introduces note taking as a skill which both promotes active listening and helps the student generate a record of what has been heard. In this unit, students learn the key word method for taking notes. Other note taking methods are presented in Units III and IV.

APPROPRIATE TECHNOLOGY

This unit introduces the student to the concept of appropriateness. Something that is appropriate fits the situation in which it is used. An understanding of the concept of appropriateness is central to the first seven units of this book.

PLEASE NOTE: The activities in this unit assume that your students already have some rudimentary skill in discerning "main ideas" in a paragraph or passsage. For those who lack this skill, you will need to provide instruction in this area. The skill will also be addressed in Unit III of this book.

INTRODUCTION

WHAT IS STUDY?

Studying means learning. Learning often involves listening, reading, watching, and writing. It always involves thinking.

You study in many different places and doing many different things. You can study basketball or soccer, clothes, dance, or other people. Whenever you try to learn, you are studying.

WHAT ARE STUDY SKILLS?

Study skills are ways or methods of learning. Knowing a variety of study skills and how to use them can help you become a more effective learner.

When you've developed study skills, you will be able to make better use of your time and effort. You'll become a more independent learner and problem solver. An independent learner knows which questions to ask and how to find the answers to those questions.

SCIENCE STUDY SKILLS

Some study skills are useful in all subjects. Knowing how to listen, for example, will help you learn in any class. Other skills are most useful in a particular class or subject.

When you learn science study skills, you find out how to learn science more effectively. For example, you discover how to read graphs and charts, how to take notes from your science textbook, and how to work with large numbers and the metric system.

People learn study skills best when they practice them. Each unit in this book will help you learn about useful study skills and will give you a chance to practice those skills.

PEOPLE, ENERGY, AND APPROPRIATE TECHNOLOGY

As you practice science study skills in this book, you will also have the chance to learn about some key ideas in science. As you examine the connections among people, energy, and technology, think about these questions:

Where does energy come from, and how is it used?
What makes one technology better, or more appropriate, than another?
How can people make the best use of the energy and technology available to them?

By the time you finish this book, you should be able to answer these questions and more about people, energy, and appropriate technology.

1

Suggested Directions for Unit I

1. Organize your class into small groups of three or four students. Have a student or students read the Introduction (page 1) aloud. Discuss for emphasis.

   Approximate time: 5 minutes

UNIT I: LISTENING AS A SCIENCE SKILL
and
WHAT DOES APPROPRIATE MEAN?

WHAT IS LISTENING?

What is *listening?* And what is the difference between listening and hearing?

You probably spend a lot of your time listening. In fact, students are asked to listen about 55% of the time that they are in school.

Think for a few moments about what you actually do when someone asks you to listen. Then, define *hearing* and *listening* on the lines below.

hearing = *a physical process in which the ears perceive sound*

listening = *hearing, paying attention to what you're hearing, and trying to make sense of it*

(Accept any reasonable answer.)

2

NOTE: The picture is an example of inappropriateness. You can discuss the picture with students at this point in the unit, asking them what seems wrong with it, or you can come back to it later in the unit after students have become more familiar with the terms appropriate and inappropriate.

2. Ask your students to read "What Is Listening?" (page 2) and answer the question at the end. Or, ask them to read the section, discuss the differences between "hearing" and "listening" in their groups, and write down the answers which they generate. When they are done, have several individuals read their own or their group's answers. Discuss, focusing on listening as an active, meaning-seeking process.

10 minutes

3. Have your students read "Listening Is A Skill" (page 3) and "Active Listening" (page 3). Go over each of the specific listening skills for emphasis.

5–10 minutes

4. Ask students to read the directions for Exercise I (page 3). Then, read aloud the paragraph for Exercise I. Give students an opportunity to write the main idea, and then have several students share their main ideas with the class. Discuss.

10 minutes

PARAGRAPH FOR EXERCISE I

It is important to choose the right tool for the task you want to do. You wouldn't use an axe to cut your meat. You wouldn't wear long underwear on a hot summer day. You wouldn't use a hammer to swat a mosquito. You would choose the equipment which best fits what you are doing. In this book, you are going to learn how to choose appropriate tools for the tasks you want to do.

EXERCISE II

Directions: You will hear three different paragraphs about the same topic. Listen carefully, and try to find the theme or main idea common to all three paragraphs.

When you have heard all three paragraphs, work with your group to describe the theme or main idea shared by the three paragraphs. Then, write the theme on the lines below.

You may want to jot down key words as you listen to help you remember. Use the space at the bottom of the page.

Theme/main idea: _(Accept any reasonable answer.) The point of these paragraphs is to introduce the concept of appropriateness. If appropriate choices and technologies had been made, energy and money could have been saved._

Key words: *(Student answers will vary.)*

4

5. Select three students in each group to be readers. Give one reader in each group passage A, one passage B, and the third passage C (on the next page), so that each group can hear all three passages. YOU WILL NEED TO DUPLICATE THE PASSAGES FOR THE READERS PRIOR TO CLASS. Tell the readers to read their passages slowly and clearly but only once.

Have the class read the directions for Exercise II (page 4). Then, tell the readers to begin.

When students have completed the exercise, have each group write its main idea on the board. Discuss the ideas, focusing on ways in which they are similar and different. Also, ask your students if they wrote down key words while they listened and in what ways this note taking helped. You may also want to go over the key words which students have written down.

15–20 minutes

PASSAGES FOR EXERCISE II

PASSAGE A

Mr. Johnson always believed in competing with his neighbor, Ms. Jackson. Ms. Jackson had just installed three solar panels on her home to provide her and her family of four with hot water. Mr. Johnson decided to buy and install six solar panels to help provide hot water for himself and his wife. "If three panels save the Jacksons some money on their fuel bill, six panels should save me twice as much," Mr. Johnson thought.

At the end of the winter, Mr. Johnson took his utility bills over to Ms. Jackson's to compare their savings. To his complete surprise, he found that his six solar panels had not saved him much more than the Jacksons' three solar panels had helped them save. "Didn't you know," Ms. Jackson said, "less than one solar panel per person is all you need?"

PASSAGE B

Joe Caruso was a contractor who specialized in building shopping centers. When he built the Riverside Shopping Center, he followed most of the usual building procedures. For example, all of the windows in the shopping center were sealed shut. This meant that even on mild days the air conditioning had to be on to keep the shopping center from overheating. One spring day the air conditioning broke down. Store owners tried to open windows but couldn't. When the shopping center manager called Mr. Caruso for advice, he had none to offer. The shopping center was forced to close until the air conditioning could be fixed.

PASSAGE C

It was Jack's turn to do the laundry, but he really did not want to do it today. He wanted to be outside enjoying the warm spring weather. Instead he was stuck in the house. He washed the clothes, threw them in the dryer, and waited for them to be done. When they were finished, more than an hour of the beautiful day had been lost. Jack put the clothes where his sister would fold them when she came home. Then he ran out into the yard, nearly catching his neck on the clothesline as he ran by.

TAKING NOTES

Taking notes is another way of becoming an active listener. To take useful notes, you need to pay attention to what you are hearing and think about what is worth writing down. When you take notes, you also create a record of what you have heard which you can use later.

One way to take notes is to write down *key words*. The steps for taking notes in this way are listed below:

1. Do not try to write down everything that you hear. Instead, listen for words which seem key or important, and jot these down. The speaker may define a key word, emphasize it, repeat it, give examples of it, or tell you in some other way to pay attention to it.

2. As you listen to a speaker, jot down all the key words that you hear. *Remember:* Key words can be a single word or a group of words.

3. When the speaker is finished, go back to each key word and write something about it. Define it, use it in a sentence, and/or give examples of it. When you write about the key words, you make sure that you really understand what they mean.

EXERCISE III

Directions: Your teacher will read a passage to you. Listen carefully, and take notes by jotting down key words on the lines below.

When your teacher is finished, write what is important about each key word. Then describe the main idea of the passage in the space provided below.

Key words: *Students' lists of key words will vary, as will what they write about them. Accept any reasonable answers. Examples of key words:*
inappropriate
appropriate
fits (the situation)
does the job
does too little, too much

Main idea: *Something which is appropriate fits the situation in which you use it.*

5

---

6. Have your students read "Taking Notes" (page 5). Go over the steps in the note taking procedure. Then, ask your students to read the directions for Exercise III (page 5). Ask them to do this exercise individually. Read the passage on the next page aloud and give them time to work with the key words and write the main idea. When they are done, have students share their key words and what they have written about them either in small groups or with the whole class. Then, discuss the main idea of the passage.

10–15 minutes

PASSAGE FOR EXERCISE III

Anything which is appropriate fits the situation. Air conditioning is appropriate only when there is no other way to keep a room or building from overheating. Remember the windows that couldn't be opened, even on mild days. An activity can be appropriate or inappropriate as well. Swimming is most appropriate for a hot summer day but not suitable for a cold winter night. Equipment can be appropriate or not. An electric knife on a camping trip where there is no electricity is just extra baggage. A folding jackknife which you can slip into your pocket would be appropriate. Behavior can also be appropriate or inappropriate. Loud yelling would be much more appropriate at a football game than in a hospital.

Anything which is not appropriate, or inappropriate, does not fit the situation. You would be surprised to see someone wearing a fur coat to go swimming, hunting butterflies in the snow, or turning cartwheels in a china shop. All of these are inappropriate.

To see if something is appropriate, ask yourself:

Does it do the job?
Does it do too little or too much?
Is there anything which fits the situation better?

If it does the job well, not by too little or too much, and if there is nothing which fits the situation better, then it is appropriate.

EXERCISE IV

Directions: Imagine that your science class is planning a day trip to the beach to examine the plants and animals which live there. In the space provided below, write three things it would be appropriate for you to bring, and three things that would be inappropriate for you to bring. On the line next to each object, explain why the object is appropriate or inappropriate for this trip.

Appropriate objects   **Why they are appropriate**

1. _____ *(Students' answers will vary.)* _____

2. _____   _____

3. _____   _____

Inappropriate objects   **Why they are inappropriate**

4. _____   _____

5. _____   _____

6. _____   _____

6

7. Assign Exercise IV (page 6) to students for homework. Read the directions aloud to students and check to see if there are any questions.

When students return to class with this assignment, have them share some of their ideas with the class. Discuss why the objects they have chosen are either appropriate or inappropriate.

10–15 minutes (for discussion)

UNIT I SUMMARY

LISTENING AND TAKING NOTES

Listening is a study skill which involves paying attention to what you are hearing and trying to make sense of it.

A good listener is an *active listener*. Active listening means *concentrating* and *participating*.

Concentrating is choosing to direct your attention to what you are hearing, and choosing to keep listening if your attention wanders.

Participating is thinking about what the speaker is saying. To participate:

1. Ask yourself questions about what you are hearing, and answer them if you can.

2. Try to connect what you are hearing with what you already know.

3. Try to "picture" in your mind what is being said.

Taking notes is another way of listening actively. One way to take notes is to jot down key words in these ways:

1. Listen for words which seem important or key, and jot them down.

2. When the speaker is finished, go back to each key word and define it, use it in a sentence, or give an example of it.

WHAT DOES APPROPRIATE MEAN?

Anything which is appropriate fits the situation in which you use it. To see if something is appropriate, ask yourself:

Does it do the job and/or fit the situation?
Does it do too little or too much?
Is there anything that fits the situation better?

If it fits the job well, not by too little or too much, and if there is nothing which fits the situation better, then it is appropriate.

7

8. Review the Summary of Unit I (page 7) with students. Point out to students that they will be tested on Units I–VII in Unit VIII and that they will want to review unit summaries periodically.

UNIT II: BUILDING YOUR SCIENCE VOCABULARY
and
WHAT MAKES A TECHNOLOGY APPROPRIATE?

STUDY SKILLS

The language of science consists of unique words and meanings. Even if students are familiar with the words they read in their science materials, they may not know the particular meanings which relate to scientific topics.

This unit is designed to improve your students' vocabulary in two ways. First, it introduces them to the skill of using context clues to decode unfamiliar words. Second, it encourages students to use a glossary or dictionary when a more precise meaning is called for or insufficient context clues exist.

APPROPRIATE TECHNOLOGY

Unit II builds on the previous unit by having students apply the idea of appropriateness to technology. Technology is the use of methods, systems, tools, and/or machines to accomplish a task.

Appropriate technology is a fairly new concept, although examples of its use can be found throughout history. By stressing small scale, cooperative approaches to problem solving on a local level, appropriate technologies involve people more directly in meeting their own basic needs for food, energy, shelter, waste disposal, and transportation. The use of appropriate technologies can also foster the development of self-esteem and community self-reliance.

UNIT II: BUILDING YOUR SCIENCE VOCABULARY
and
WHAT MAKES A TECHNOLOGY APPROPRIATE?

INTRODUCTION

In your reading you will often come across words that you don't know.

Read the paragraph written below. Then, try to define each of the underlined words in the space provided beneath the paragraph. You're not expected to know all of the words. Just do the best you can!

The concepts of environment and ecosystem have been around for a long time. But only in the past few years have these ideas become familiar to most people. People have begun to realize that all living things depend on the ecosystem to which they belong. For living things to sustain themselves, they require a healthy environment.

ecosystem _community of living things_

sustain _stay alive_

LEARNING NEW WORDS

You may not have known the exact meanings of the words underlined in the paragraph above. Yet you were probably able to figure out a meaning for each word that helped you make sense of the paragraph.

Science has its own vocabulary or set of words. To understand what is going on in science, you need to know what the words mean. In this unit, you will learn two ways to find out the meanings of new words.

CONTEXT CLUES

You may have figured out the meaning of a new word in the paragraph above by thinking about the words and sentences around it. This is called getting the meaning from CONTEXT CLUES.

A CONTEXT is the setting in which something is found. For example, a jewelry store is a context in which rings are sold. A circus is a context where you would expect to find clowns and trapezes.

When you read, the CONTEXT is the words and sentences around a particular word. These familiar words and sentences, called CONTEXT CLUES, can often help you figure out the meaning of a word you do not recognize.

Example: Some sources of energy we now use will not last forever. For example, because the amount of oil left in the ground is finite, we have to find other sources of energy before it runs out.

finite means: _having a definite end_

8

Suggested Directions for Unit II

1. Organize your class into groups of three or four students.

2. Read the "Introduction" (page 8) aloud or have a student read it aloud. Ask students to work in their groups to define the two words listed beneath the paragraphs. When they have finished, have one student from each group read the group's definition. Ask students how they knew or figured out the meaning of each word.

Approximate time: 5-10 minutes

3. Have students read "Learning New Words" and "Context Clues" (page 8). Go over the meaning of context and context clues. Ask students to read the Example (page 8) and define the word *finite* using context clues given. Discuss what clues they used to define *finite*.

5-10 minutes

4. Ask students to read the directions for Exercise I (page 9). Then, read aloud the two paragraphs called "Appropriate Technology" which are a part of the exercise. Have students complete Exercise I in their groups. When they are done, have several students share their context clues and definitions with the class.

15 minutes

5. Ask students to read the directions for Exercise II (page 9). Have them read through the rest of the passage on appropriate technology (page 10), underlining words they do not know. Once they have finished the story, the directions tell them to try to define each underlined word. When the groups are done, have them share their words and definitions with the rest of the class. You may want to make a class list of words and definitions for later use.

15 minutes

APPROPRIATE TECHNOLOGY (continued)

Like Michael and Maria Lopez, we all need food on a daily basis in order to remain strong and healthy. Unfortunately, most of us depend on a network of people and services spread out all across the country to keep us from going hungry. For example, acres of wheat are grown by farmers in the Midwest, and then harvested, transported, milled into flour, and transported again, finally to appear as bread on your table. Many of the fruits and vegetables you enjoy are grown in the other states and shipped to you in refrigerated trucks.

In the last few years this nationwide food supply network has become more vulnerable and expensive. Insects, lack of rain, strikes by farm workers and truckers, problems with highways, and energy shortages have all contributed to temporary food shortages and higher prices at the market. Winter storms, floods, and earthquakes could have an even more damaging effect in the future. Clearly, we need a more reliable system for feeding the nation. We can use appropriate technology to help find better ways to meet this basic human need.

Boston Urban Gardeners (BUG) is an example of people using appropriate technology to meet their own basic need for food. By using vacant lots from all over the city, making and using compost piles, and calling on the talents and enthusiasm of its members as well as other local resources, BUG has given people control over the production of their own summer vegetables.

Underlined words   **Definitions**

_____   _____
_____   _____
_____   _____
_____   _____
_____   _____

A FOOD NETWORK

10

NOTE: The illustration on page 10 may be discussed with students as an example of a food network.

14

LEARNING NEW WORDS: USING THE GLOSSARY

Sometimes you may not be able to find enough context clues to help you define a word you do not know. Or you may need to know the exact meaning of a word in order to understand the sentence or paragraph in which it appears. Science textbooks often have a small dictionary of new words at the end, called a GLOSSARY, which defines some of these words for you.

A GLOSSARY does not give you as much information about a word as a dictionary would, but it will give you the exact meaning of a word as your science book uses it. Using the GLOSSARY is a convenient way to learn new words as you read.

EXERCISE III

Directions: Below is a list of words from the "Appropriate Technology" story. Find each word in the Glossary on page 119. Write the definition given for each word on the line next to it.

Then, below each word, write a sentence or two in which you use the new word. In your sentences, try to include context clues which would help another person define the word.

Example: ___daily___   ___every day___

Sentence: Ann weeded the garden daily, because every day there were new weeds growing among the vegetables.

1. appropriate technology   _methods of meeting needs that fit the situation_

    Sentence: _(Students' answers will vary.)_

2. local _nearby_

    Sentence: _____

(Continued on page 12)

11

6. Have students read "Learning New Words: Using The Glossary" (page 11). Ask them to turn to the glossary on page 117, and discuss what information is found in a glossary and how they can best use it.

    5–10 minutes

7. Ask students to read the directions for Exercise III (page 11), and have them begin working. This exercise can be done individually or in groups. When students have finished, have them share the sentences they have written within their small groups or with the class.

    10–15 minutes

3. resources ___*a supply of something available for use*___

    Sentence: _____

    _____

    _____

4. disposal ___*throwing away or getting rid of something*___

    Sentence: _____

    _____

    _____

5. crisis ___*a time of danger or difficulty*___

    Sentence: _____

    _____

    _____

EXERCISE IV

Directions: Below is a list of resources you use at home. We can get and dispose of these resources using technologies which are appropriate or inappropriate.

To the left of this list are spaces where you can check off where the resource comes from. To the right of the list, you can check off where you dispose, or get rid of, each resource.

Complete as much of this chart as you can, checking off where each resource comes from and how you dispose of it. You may need to ask your parents for help. You can also check package labels to find out where a resource comes from.

Do the best you can. If you do not use one of the resources listed in your home, or can't find out about where it comes from or how you dispose of it, leave that part of the chart blank.

HOME RESOURCE USE CHECKLIST

WHERE RESOURCE IS PRODUCED					WHERE YOU DISPOSE OF RESOURCE			
Locally	In Your State	In United States	In Another Country	RESOURCE USED AT HOME	Dump	Sewer	Burn	Recycle
				Eggs				
				Meat				
				Bread				
				Dairy products				
				Fruits/vegetables				
				Plastic bottles				
				Glass bottles				
				Aluminum cans				
				Newspaper				
				Fertilizer				
				Water				
				Electricity				
				Gasoline				
				Oil				
				Coal				
				Natural gas/propane				
				Solar energy				

13

8. Have students read the directions for Exercise IV (page 13). Explain that students will complete the checklist in Exercise IV as homework. Go over the sections of the chart students are to fill in. Suggest that they ask their parents for help, and explain that they may not be able to complete the entire chart. We recommend that this be an ungraded homework assignment, and that the information students collect be used to create a single classroom chart that summarizes their findings, or as the basis of a discussion about appropriate technology in the home.

15–20 minutes (for follow-up discussion)

17

UNIT II SUMMARY

LEARNING NEW WORDS IN SCIENCE

You will often come across new words when reading your science materials. Two ways of finding out what these words mean are using *context clues* and using the *glossary* of terms in your science book.

> *Context clues* are familiar words and phrases in a sentence or paragraph. From these words, you can often figure out the meaning of an unknown word.

> The *glossary* is a small dictionary in your science book. It provides you with the exact meaning of the word as it is used in your book.

APPROPRIATE TECHNOLOGY

Technologies are the methods, systems, tools, and machines we use to accomplish a task.

Appropriate technologies:

- use local talents and resources,
- can be understood, created, operated, and repaired by the people who depend on them,
- are usually smaller and less expensive than more complicated technologies.

Communities can use appropriate technologies to solve their own problems and meet their basic needs.

14

---

9. Review the Unit II Summary (page 14) with students.

Additional Suggestions

1. Have students list local resources which could be or are now being used to meet their community's needs. Have them explain how each resource could be or is being used. For example, crop and kitchen waste could be used for composting; backyards and garden spaces are suitable for gardening; and sunlight, wind, falling water, forests, coal, and natural gas deposits may be locally available sources of energy.

2. Have students investigate one or more of the local resources described in their homework or the activity above. Students could find out: Who would they talk to about developing its use? What else do they need to know? How will they find out about it?

UNIT III: READING FOR MEANING
and
PETROLEUM: HOW LONG WILL IT LAST?

STUDY SKILLS

Units III and IV introduce your students to several skills for reading science materials and taking notes about them. Most students faced with a reading assignment begin with the first word of the text and read for as long as their interest or sense of duty carries them. Students rarely approach their reading with a systematic plan for learning from what they read.

Unit III provides students with a four-step process which will help them become more efficient and effective readers. Each of the steps and its value to students is explained below.

1. SURVEYING: Skimming the title, introduction, subheadings, and conclusion of a reading alerts students to what the reading is about and prepares them for the details which follow.

2. READING: This step includes identifying the *main idea* or ideas presented in the reading and the details which support those ideas. Reading for the purpose of identifying *main ideas* and *supporting details* focuses students' attention as they read.

3. MAPPING: Mapping is a method of taking notes that allows students to represent the main idea and supporting details of the reading in a graphic or pictorial way. Many students find that mapping is an effective way for them to organize information from which they can study, although some of your students may prefer outlining, presented in Unit IV. Mapping is an alternative method of note taking which is also useful to students in class discussions or presentations in which there is no clear organization, because it allows them to draw connections between ideas as they arise.

4. CHECKING: Students can check themselves on what they have learned in several ways, such as summarizing the reading, asking and answering questions, and discussing specific points with others. Checking helps students pull together the most important information in a reading and put it into words which are meaningful to them.

A NOTE ABOUT TEACHING METHODS

We suggest that you have students work in groups as you introduce these skills. Working in groups lets students try out the new skills with the help of others. When students have experienced some success in using four-step method, you can structure assignments which ask them to use the steps on their own as they read.

NON-RENEWABLE ENERGY

More than 90 percent of the energy currently consumed in the U.S. comes from non-renewable sources. Non-renewable means those resources which are consumed faster than they are replaced. Non-renewable resources include coal, oil, and natural gas deposits, which take millions of years to be replaced by decaying plants. Other non-renewable resources are uranium, geothermal, and some forms of hydropower.

Unit III presents students with the picture of the planet Earth, and the U.S. in particular, consuming its limited non-renewable energy supply at a startling rate. In the past hundred years, for example, we have used more than half of the world's estimated supply of petroleum, which took more than a million years to form. A proven reserve of a resource is the portion of a known deposit which is profitable to extract, refine, and sell. While our proven reserves of petroleum have remained fairly constant in recent years, our current rates of petroleum consumption indicate the eventual exhaustion of our supplies.*

Unit IV will suggest the alternative use of renewable energy sources such as sun, wind, and water.

You may need to keep the following ideas in mind in teaching about non-renewable energy:

1. Conflicting numbers: The federal government and coal, oil, and natural gas companies all publish information about energy. Although the government often relies on these companies for its information, numbers may vary from source to source. We suggest that you rely on statistics published by the government.

2. Updating information: We suggest that you update the numbers used in the readings in Units III and IV each year. This will also allow you to check the accuracy of the forecasts referred to in the units. One source for updating these numbers is the National Information Center of the Office of Energy Information: (202) 252-8800. The figures used in this unit come from the July, 1981 *Monthly Energy Review* and the 1979 *International Energy Annual,* both of which were published by the Energy Information Administration, a branch of the U.S. Department of Energy.

3. Other fossil fuels: Information needed to rewrite the passages in this unit so that they focus on coal or natural gas rather than oil can be found in Appendix A.

*See Appendix A for an explanation of the derivation of the figures on U.S. reserves as of January, 1982.

UNIT III: READING FOR MEANING
and PETROLEUM: HOW LONG WILL IT LAST?

INTRODUCTION

Your science teacher often asks you to read through a chapter or some other materials on your own. A good way to start is to SURVEY the reading.

To SURVEY a reading:
- look at the *title* of the reading,
- look at the *headings* and *subheadings* throughout the reading, which are usually in darker or larger print than the rest of the reading,
- read the *introduction* and *conclusion* or summary, or the first and last paragraphs of the reading. If you are surveying a paragraph, read the first and last sentences.

By SURVEYING a reading before you read it, you can usually find out what it is about and what its main points are. Surveying prepares your mind to take in the details presented in the main text of the reading.

EXERCISE I

Directions: Your teacher will give you 2–3 minutes to *survey* this unit, "Reading for Meaning," using the steps listed above.

After you have surveyed this unit, use the space below to write three things you expect to learn from reading the unit.

I EXPECT TO LEARN:

1. _Students' answers will vary. Possible answers include:_
   how to read for meaning; how to take mapped notes;
   about the energy crisis; about non-renewable energy;
2. _how to check after reading._

3. _____

15

Suggested Directions for Unit III

1. Organize your class into groups of three or four students.

2. Ask students to read the "Introduction" (page 15), or read it aloud as they follow along. Discuss as necessary.
   Approximate time: 5 minutes

3. Have students read the directions for Exercise I (page 15). Give students two or three minutes to survey the unit individually, and then ask the groups to generate what they expect to learn. Discuss their responses.
   10 minutes

READING FOR MEANING: FOUR STEPS

One way of becoming a more effective reader of science books and articles is to use a set of four steps which help you find the most important points in the reading. You have already practiced the first step, SURVEYING, in the Introduction to this unit and in Exercise I.

The four steps of reading for meaning which you will learn in this chapter are:

SURVEY

READ

MAP

CHECK

READING: MAIN IDEAS AND SUPPORTING DETAILS

Once you have surveyed a reading, the second step in reading for meaning is to READ. As you read, you need to identify the *main ideas* and *supporting details* of each paragraph or section.

The MAIN IDEA is the most important idea of the paragraph or section. The rest of the paragraph or section is built around this central idea. The main idea is often, but not always, contained in the first sentence of the paragraph or section.

SUPPORTING DETAILS explain, prove, or tell something about the main idea of the paragraph or section. They make the main idea clearer or give more information about it.

Identifying main ideas and supporting details as you read will help you remember the important information in your science reading.

Example: Find the main idea and supporting details in this paragraph:

Boston Urban Gardeners (BUG) is an example of people using appropriate technology to meet their own basic need for food. By using vacant lots from all over the city, making and using compost piles, and calling on the talents and enthusiasm of its members as well as other local resources, BUG has given people control over the production of their own summer vegetables.

Main idea: ___*BUG helps people use appropriate technology to produce*___
___*their own food.*___

Supporting details: ___*locally used resources include:*___
___*— vacant lots, compost piles, members' talents*___

EXERCISE II

Directions: Survey and then read the passage "Spaceship Earth" given on the next page. In the space provided, write the main idea of each paragraph and list the details which support that main idea.

16

---

4. Have students read "Reading For Meaning: Four Steps" and "Reading: Main Ideas And Supporting Details" (page 16). Read the example (page 16) aloud, and ask students to identify the main idea and supporting details in it.

   5–10 minutes

5. Have students read the directions for Exercise II (page 16) and complete the exercise in their groups. Discuss their responses when they have finished.

   10–15 minutes

SPACESHIP EARTH

When a spaceship blasts off it must carry all the fuel it needs for its entire voyage. But the amount of fuel it can carry is limited. Like a spaceship, the planet Earth has a limited amount of fuel available for use.

Over 90% of the energy used in the U.S. today comes from finite sources within the earth, such as coal, natural gas, and petroleum. To make matters worse, we are using them up faster than new deposits can form. For example, it takes more than one million years for decaying plants and animals to become petroleum. In the last one hundred years, we have used more than half of the known world supply of petroleum. No one knows for sure when we will run out of non-renewable sources of energy, such as coal, oil, and natural gas, but some people predict that it will happen within your lifetime.

Paragraph 1

Main idea: _The earth is like a spaceship._

Supporting details: _— spaceship has limited fuel_
— Earth has limited supply of energy

Paragraph 2

Main idea: _We are using up energy sources faster than they can_
be replaced.

Supporting details: _— most energy we use is non-renewable_
— takes 1 million years for plants and animals
to become petroleum
— in last 100 years we've used up more than half of world's petroleum
— some experts say we will run out of energy in my lifetime.

"Be sure we have enough   we don't want to run out between here and Mars."

17

MAPPING

The third step in reading for meaning in science is taking notes. Taking notes helps you to keep track of the main ideas and supporting details you identify as you read.

MAPPING is one way to take notes about what you read. To make a map of your reading:

- Find the main idea. Write it down and circle it.

- As you identify supporting details, write them on lines connected to your main idea circle.

Your map will look something like this:

When you are done, your map will remind you of the most important points in your reading.

Example: Below is one student's map of the second paragraph of "Spaceship Earth."

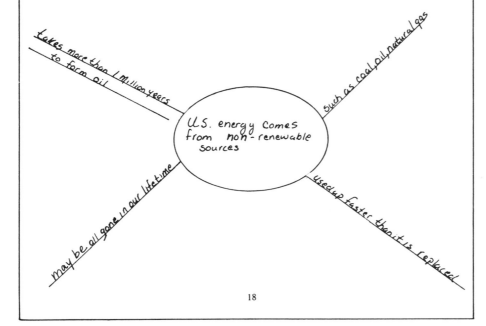

18

6. Read "Mapping" (page 18) aloud to your students, or have a student read it aloud. Have students look at the example (page 18) of mapped notes of a paragraph from the "Spaceship Earth" reading. Discuss and clarify this method of note taking with your students. You may want to map the other paragraph of "Spaceship Earth" with your students if you feel they need more clarification.

5–10 minutes

24

7. Have students read the directions for Exercise III (page 19) and complete the exercise in their
groups. When they have finished, ask two or three students from different groups to put their
completed maps on the board. Discuss similarities and differences.

15 minutes

CHECKING

When you have surveyed, read, and mapped a reading, the final step is to CHECK what you have learned. CHECKING helps you remember the most important points in the reading.

You can CHECK yourself in the following ways:

    1) Ask yourself, "What is the most important idea(s) I have learned from this reading?"

    2) Discuss the reading with other people who have read it.

EXERCISE IV

Directions: Re-read the first two paragraphs of "The Energy Crisis" on page 19. Then, read the next two paragraphs below. In the space provided on the next page, 1) *map* the last two paragraphs, and 2) *check* yourself on what you have learned by writing two or three sentences that explain the most important ideas from "The Energy Crisis."

THE ENERGY CRISIS *(continued)*

Each year the U.S. uses about three billion barrels of its own oil. In 1980 we pumped 3.14 billion barrels of petroleum out of the ground. In 1981 we pumped 3.13 billion barrels, and in 1982 we removed another 3.16 billion barrels. According to U.S. government figures, our proven reserves, or the amount of petroleum left in the ground which can be sold at a profit, had shrunk to only 29.4 billion barrels by January 1, 1982.

If we continue to use about 3 billion barrels of our own petroleum each year without increasing our proven reserves, they will be gone by 1992. Of course, the discovery of new petroleum in the U.S. goes on. These new reserves are added to our proven reserves, making it unlikely that we will actually run out of petroleum in 1992.

Yet the supply of domestic petroleum, a non-renewable resource, is limited. Many people believe that the U.S. will run out of petroleum within the next several decades. At that point we will either have to depend on other countries for oil or substitute other forms of energy.

20

8. Have students read "Checking" (page 20) to themselves. Discuss student questions or comments. Ask students to read the directions to Exercise IV (page 20) and to complete the exercise in their groups. When students have finished, ask one student from each group to report their summary to the class.

15 minutes

1. MAP of these two paragraphs: *Student answers will vary. Below is one possible map and summary or check*

Only 29.4 billion barrels left

pumped 3.14 billion barrels in 1980

U.S. running out of oil

pumped 3.13 billion barrels in 1981

By 1992, U.S. oil will be gone

pumped 3.16 billion barrels in 1982

2. CHECK on "The Energy Crisis": *The 1973 energy crisis made us aware of our dependence on other countries for oil. The U.S. plan to reduce this dependence won't work because there isn't enough oil left in the U.S. to meet our energy needs past 1992 if we continue our present rate of use.*

21

UNIT III SUMMARY

READING FOR MEANING

The four step method of reading for meaning will help you learn and remember more from your science readings. All four steps ask you to think about the *main ideas,* or most important points, in the reading, and the *supporting details* which back up those points.

To read for meaning:

SURVEY: Look quickly over the titles, introduction, headings, and conclusion, or first and last paragraphs or sentences. Surveying tells you what the main ideas of a reading are.

READ: As you read, focus on the main ideas and supporting details.

MAP: Make a map that shows the main ideas and supporting details. A map helps you keep track of important information as you read. It also gives you notes you can use later.

CHECK: Look over your mapped notes and remind yourself what this reading is about. Ask yourself, "What have I learned from this reading?"

NON-RENEWABLE ENERGY

Most of the energy we use today comes from non-renewable sources such as coal, petroleum, and natural gas.

NON-RENEWABLE means that we use these sources much faster than they re-form within the earth. We could use up our proven reserves of all of these limited energy sources within 100 years if we continue to depend on them for all of our energy needs. (A proven reserve is the amount of a natural resource which can be mined, processed, and sold at a profit.)

22

9. Review the "Unit III Summary" (page 22) with your students.

UNIT IV: TAKING EFFECTIVE NOTES
and
SUN, WIND, AND WATER: HOPE FOR THE FUTURE?

STUDY SKILLS

Each of your students learns about and understands the world in his or her own way. Each learning situation may require the student to use different study skills. For these reasons it is important to present students with a variety of study skills from which they can choose. Students can learn to judge which skill or skills they are most comfortable using and which skills are most appropriate to a particular learning situation. In this way, students can become more effective learners.

This unit introduces students to two more note taking skills, OUTLINING and making DATA TABLES. While mapping, presented in Unit III, might be more effective for students who tend to learn best in a pictorial, holistic mode, outlining may be useful for students who prefer sequentially organized information. Also, students may prefer to use outlining to take notes from highly organized reading materials or presentations.

A DATA TABLE combines the orderliness of outlining with the visual connection of ideas found in mapping. Data tables help students organize large amounts of information so that patterns in the data emerge. By making data tables, students can begin to see the "whole picture" as well as the way in which each part fits.

RENEWABLE ENERGY

Unlike the finite fossil fuels, renewable energy supplies are replaced nearly as fast as they are used. Unit IV introduces the sources of renewable energy and examines how they can be used to address the energy concerns raised in Unit III.

Most renewable energy sources draw on the power of the sun in some way. The following sources are discussed in this unit.

Thermal solar energy is the direct use of the sun's energy to heat air and water. Solar energy is used *actively* when electric fans or pumps are used to transfer it to where it is used or stored. It is used *passively* when no electrical or mechanical assistance is employed.

Photovoltaics is the conversion of the sun's rays into electricity when they strike a photovoltaic cell commonly made from thin wafers of silicon. When energized particles of light called photons strike the silicon, they knock electrons loose. The electrons flow into connecting wires, creating a current of electricity.

Wind is the movement of air from high to low pressure areas created by the unequal heating of the earth by the sun. *Wind power* can be tapped by putting a sail or blade in the path of this moving air. As the wind pushes against this barrier, it causes an axle to turn. The resulting energy can be used to perform mechanical work such as pumping water or turning an electric generator.

Hydropower results from water falling onto a paddle wheel or blade. Often, water falling from high to low elevations comes from moisture evaporated from oceans and lakes by the sun and deposited at higher elevations when it rains. As the falling water turns an axle, the energy it produces can be used to generate electricity or to perform mechanical work. It is important to note that although the falling water is renewable, dams built to harness hydropower have a life expectancy of 50 to 200 years.

Biomass is the energy stored in growing things. Whenever vegetation receives solar energy, the process of photosynthesis locks it away in the chemical bonds needed to form carbohydrates. Wood, garbage, and other plant materials can be burned or converted into methane, a burnable gas, or into alcohol, a liquid fuel.

In 1979, a report published by the Solar Energy Research Institute (SERI) concluded that energy conservation and renewable resources could play crucial roles in America's energy future. The report says that imaginative use of available technologies to improve the productivity of fuels in short supply along with widespread adoption of technologies which use renewable resources constitutes the cheapest, fastest, and safest strategy for rebuilding our country's energy base over the next 20 years.

UNIT IV: TAKING EFFECTIVE NOTES
and
SUN, WIND, AND WATER: HOPE FOR THE FUTURE?

INTRODUCTION

In Unit III you learned that mapping helps you keep track of the important information as you read. Your map also gives you a record of the reading which you can study later.

This unit will show you two other ways to take notes, OUTLINING and making DATA TABLES.

After you have used all three forms of note taking for some time, you may find that one seems to work best for you. You may also find that each way of taking notes is more useful at some times than others.

To discover the best way for *you* to take notes in science, you need to experiment with several ways. This unit will help you do that.

NOTE TAKING TIPS

You have already learned several important skills which will help you take notes.

1. KEY WORDS — You don't need to write your notes in complete sentences. Write only the key words and phrases which tell you the main idea and important details.

2. MAIN IDEAS AND SUPPORTING DETAILS — Take notes only on the main ideas and important details. Don't try to write down everything in the reading.

Remember: Your notes are for you! Take notes *in your own words,* so that they make sense to you. You may want to use some key words from the reading, but be sure you understand what your notes say.

23

Suggested Directions for Unit IV

1. Read the "Introduction" (page 23) aloud, or have a student read it aloud. Discuss the idea that there is no one right way to take notes. Different note taking methods may be best for different students and for various learning situations.

Read "Note Taking Tips" (page 23) aloud, or have students read it aloud. Discuss each tip as necessary.

Approximate time: 5 minutes

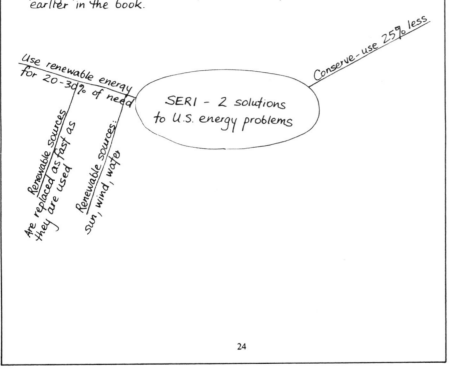
2. Organize your class into pairs. Ask students to read the directions for Exercise I (page 24) and to complete the exercise with their partners. When they have finished, have two or three students put their maps on the board. Discuss the results.

10 minutes

OUTLINING

Sometimes mapping is not the most useful way to organize your notes. OUTLINING is a way of taking notes that shows the order of events or details as they appear in your reading. The form for outlining is shown below.

OUTLINE FORM

I. Main idea

    A. Supporting detail
    B. Supporting detail
    C. Supporting detail

II. Main idea

STEPS FOR OUTLINING

Follow the steps below for taking notes in outline form.

1. Identify the main idea and supporting details of a reading or paragraph.

2. Use a Roman numeral to list the main idea.

3. Use capital letters to list the details which explain or support that main idea. Indent each capital letter to the right of the Roman numeral to set it off from the main idea.

4. Repeat as needed.

Example: Below is an outline of the paragraph you just read and mapped about "Renewable Energy."

    I. SERI found ways to stop U.S. oil imports by 2000

        A. Conserve energy – save 25%

        B. Use renewable energy sources for 20% to 30% of what we need

EXERCISE II

Directions: Read the rest of the passage on renewable energy on the next page. Write your notes about the reading in OUTLINE FORM in the space provided after the reading. Parts of the outline have been filled in for you.

25

3. Read "Outlining" and "Steps For Outlining" (page 25) with your students. Have students look at the Example (page 25) and compare it to their maps of the same paragraph. Ask them to describe any similarities and differences they see.

5–10 minutes

4. Have students read the directions for Exercise II (page 25) and complete the exercise in pairs. When students are done, ask several to put their outlines on the board. Discuss, keeping in mind the note taking tips on page 23. Or, have each pair join another and compare the outlines they have made.

15–20 minutes

RENEWABLE ENERGY *(continued)*

What are the renewable energy sources which hold such promise? All of them use the power of the sun in one way or another. Unlike oil, coal, or natural gas, they are quickly replaced no matter how much of them we use.

Solar energy is one renewable source. Thermal solar power uses the sun's rays to produce heat for homes, offices, and schools. It can also be used to heat water. The SERI report estimates that the U.S. could collect 3.9% to 4.5% of its energy from this source by the end of the century. The sun's rays can also be turned into electricity through the use of *photovoltaics*. Photovoltaic energy could provide a little less than one percent of our energy needs by the year 2000.

The power of the *wind* can also be harnessed to produce electricity or to do mechanical work like pumping water. Wind power could supply 2% to 5% of our energy by the year 2000.

Hydropower is the energy contained in falling water. It could supply another 4.8% to 5.5% of our energy, mostly in the form of electricity.

The renewable energy source with the most potential is *biomass*. Biomass is the energy contained in growing things. Wood and garbage and other plant material can be burned to produce heat. They can also be turned into methane, a burnable gas, or into alcohol, a liquid fuel. Energy from biomass could supply 7.8% to 13.5% of our energy needs by the end of the century.

OUTLINE   *(Student outlines will vary. Below is one possible outline of this reading.)*

I.   Renewable energy

A.   *All use sun's power*

B.   *Are quickly renewed.*

II. Solar energy

A. *Thermal solar – uses sun's rays for heat and hot water; could provide 3.9 to 4.5% of our energy*

B. *Photovoltaics – turns sun's rays into electricity; can provide less than 1% of our energy needs*

III. Wind power

A. *For electricity or manual work*

B. *2-5% of our energy*

IV. Hydropower

A. *For electricity*

B. *4.8 - 5.5% of our energy*

V. Biomass

A. *Energy from growing things*   B. *Burn wood and garbage*

C. *Methane gas and alcohol from plants*   26   D. *7.8 - 13.5% of our energy*

DATA TABLES

Some readings present you with many facts about several related subjects. You may want to take notes on these readings that show connections between the facts, as mapping does, *and* that organize all the facts in an orderly way, as outlining does. One way to do this in one set of notes is to make a DATA TABLE from the reading.

A data table is a chart which shows the data or facts in the reading. An example of a data table of the third paragraph of the reading, "Renewable Energy," is shown below.

Example:

SOURCES OF RENEWABLE ENERGY

Energy sources	Uses	Possible % of U.S. energy it could provide	
		Lowest	Highest
Thermal solar power	heat, hot water	3.9%	4.5%
Photovoltaics	electricity	—	less than 1%

27

5. Read "Data Tables" and "How To Make A Data Table" (pages 27–28) with your students. As you read "How To Make A Data Table," refer back to the Example on page 27. Emphasize the uses of a data table and clarify the steps for making one.

10 minutes

HOW TO MAKE A DATA TABLE

A DATA TABLE is most useful for taking notes on readings which give you several different pieces of information about each related topic. Follow the steps below to make a data table. Look at the example on page 27 as you read through the steps.

1. On the left hand side of your paper, identify and list the *topics* about which you have several different pieces of information.

   In the *Example* on page 27, these topics are solar power and photovoltaics.

2. Along the top of your paper, write the *kinds of information* you have about each topic.

   In the *Example* on page 27, the information you have about each energy source is its use, the smallest percentage of U.S. energy needs it could supply, and the largest percentage of energy needs it could supply.

3. Draw lines between topics to make *rows* and between kinds of information to make *columns.*

4. *Fill in the information* about each topic in the appropriate boxes.

   In the *Example* on page 27, thermal solar power is used for heat and hot water, and photovoltaic power is used for electricity.

5. Give your DATA TABLE a *title* that explains what information it contains.

   The title of the data table in the *Example* is "Sources of Renewable Energy."

EXERCISE III

Directions: Re-read the last three paragraphs of "Renewable Energy" on page 26. In the space provided below, make a data table of the information in those three paragraphs.

Follow the steps listed above. Use the *Example* on page 27 as a model.

RENEWABLE ENERGY SOURCES
(title)

Energy sources	Uses	Possible % of U.S. energy it could provide	
		Lowest	Highest
Wind power	electricity mechanical work	2.0	5.0
Hydropower	electricity	4.8	5.5
Biomass	heat	7.8	13.5

28

6. Ask students to read the directions for Exercise III (page 28). Point out that the data table they will make is a continuation of the one presented in the Example on page 27. It uses the same column heads and adds three rows. Have students work in pairs to complete Exercise III. Ask several students to share their data tables with the class, or ask two pairs to compare the data tables they have made.

10 minutes

EXERCISE IV

Directions: Survey and read "Renewable Energy and Appropriate Technology" below.

In the spaces provided on the next page:

1) Take notes on the first two paragraphs in either MAP or OUTLINE form.

2) Take notes on the last three paragraphs by making a DATA TABLE of the information.

3) CHECK yourself by writing a one or two sentence summary telling what you learned from this reading.

RENEWABLE ENERGY AND APPROPRIATE TECHNOLOGY

When technologies use non-renewable sources of energy, they are limited in several ways. To begin with, oil, coal, and natural gas are usually removed from the ground in far away places, often in foreign countries. They must be shipped great distances in order to reach us. This makes them more expensive than they would be if they were available locally. Non-renewable energy sources also face shortages and sudden cutoffs which can bring the technologies dependent on them to a stop.

As non-renewable resources grow more scarce, they will become more and more expensive. One day in the not-so-distant future, the proven reserves may run out. From then on, the technologies which used them will be useless.

Appropriate technologies avoid these limitations by drawing their power from renewable energy sources whenever possible. For example, consider the differences between a house heated by a non-renewable fuel like natural gas and a similar house heated primarily by the sun. The house using natural gas for heat depends on a constant supply to stay warm. If there is a shortage of natural gas caused by a very cold winter or by a shipping problem, the gas heated house may become too cold for comfort if its supply runs out before the problem is solved. The solar heated house, on the other hand, cannot be cut off from its main fuel supply for more than a few days at a time.

The owner of the gas heated house will have to spend more and more money for natural gas every year. The cost goes up as the proven reserves of natural gas get smaller and the cost of shipping increases. In contrast, the house equipped with solar technology has small, stable energy costs. The owner of the solar heated house will only have to spend money for heat during periods of cloudy weather.

The day will come when the natural gas reserves are nearly gone. On that day the owner of the gas heated house will have to replace his or her gas fired furnace with a more appropriate technology. Chances are it will run on renewable energy.

7. Ask students to read the directions for Exercise IV (page 29). Have students complete Exercise IV with their partners. When students have finished, ask several students to share their notes with the class by putting them on the board. Or, ask pairs to compare the notes they have taken. Discuss with students their experience in using each form of note taking.

15–20 minutes

1) MAP or OUTLINE of paragraphs 1 and 2: *(Student maps and outlines will vary.)*

    OUTLINE: I. Limitations of technologies using non-renewable energy
                 A. Expensive to operate because fuels come from far away
                 B. Can be paralyzed by shortages and cutoffs
                 C. Cost of fuels go up as proven reserves get smaller
                 D. Will not work when fuel is used up

MAP:

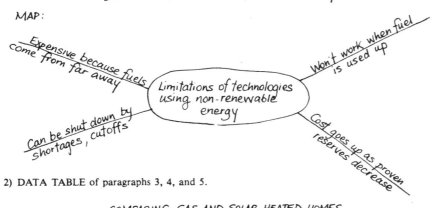

2) DATA TABLE of paragraphs 3, 4, and 5.

COMPARING GAS AND SOLAR HEATED HOMES
(title)

Kind of heat in house	Shortages and cutoffs	Costs	Future
gas	May get too cold if supply used up before problem solved.	Goes up as proven reserves shrink and transport costs go up.	Will have to switch to renewable energy when proven reserves are used up.
solar	Can't be cut off for more than a few days.	Only costs $ during periods of cloudy weather.	There will always be solar heat.

3) CHECK: <u>*(Student answers will vary.)* Appropriate technologies use renewable energy sources because they cost less, they are always available, and they will never run out.</u>

UNIT IV SUMMARY

TAKING NOTES

There is no one right way to take notes. Different note taking methods are appropriate in different situations. You may be more comfortable taking notes in a certain way.

The important part of taking notes is to record the main ideas and supporting details in a way that makes them easy for you to understand and remember.

TIPS: 1. Only write down key words and phrases, not complete sentences.

2. Take notes on main ideas and supporting details. Don't try to record everything.

3. Take notes in your own words, so that they make sense to you.

OUTLINING is a way of taking notes that shows the order in which events happened. It can also show which supporting detail comes before another. This is an OUTLINE FORM:

I. Main idea

    A. Supporting detail

    B. Supporting detail

    C. Supporting detail

II. Main idea

Making a DATA TABLE is helpful when a reading gives you several pieces of information about more than one topic. The data table shows you how each topic is the same or different from the others. A data table might look like this:

RENEWABLE ENERGY

Energy source	Uses	Advantages	Disadvantages
Thermal solar power	heat hot water	small, fixed costs usually available	
Hydropower	electricity	small, fixed costs renewable	have to be near falling water
Wind power	electricity mechanical work	small, fixed costs renewable	need wind

RENEWABLE ENERGY

The Solar Energy Research Institute (SERI) believes that the use of renewable energy is one solution to our energy problems. By the year 2000, 20% to 30% of our energy needs could be met by using renewable energy sources, of which we have a nearly unlimited supply.

The renewable energy sources with the greatest promise for the future are:

1) thermal solar energy — direct use of the sun's rays,

2) photovoltaics — using the sun to generate electricity,

3) wind power — harnassing the power of the wind,

4) hydropower — using falling water to generate energy, and

5) biomass — using the energy stored in growing things.

Appropriate technologies use renewable energy whenever possible to avoid shortages and cutoffs. Renewable energy is replaced almost as fast as it is used.

31

8. Review the Unit IV Summary (page 31) with your students.

UNIT V: MAKING JUDGMENTS
and
HOW DOES TECHNOLOGY AFFECT THE ENVIRONMENT?

STUDY SKILLS

We often ask students to make comparisons and judgments in science. Comparing and judging are complex processes which need to be broken down into simpler steps for students to master.

This unit presents students with two considerations involved in making judgments or decisions. First, students learn that they need facts in order to make sound decisions and that facts are different from opinions.

Second, students are introduced to the use of criteria to help them judge different sets of facts. They are asked to rate several energy technologies using a given list of criteria.

ENERGY AND THE ENVIRONMENT

All technologies have some impact on the environment. Appropriate technologies, however, tend to have fewer negative effects on the environment than other technologies. Environmental impact is another factor in evaluating the appropriateness of a technology.

This unit presents students with a set of criteria for judging the effects of five different home heating technologies on the environment. Students are asked to use these criteria to rate different methods of home heating. The criteria given are:

1. The technology should have minimal short and long term effects on living things.

2. The technology should not make the environment look or smell unpleasant.

3. The environment should be able to recover quickly from the impact of the technology.

4. The technology should produce little waste material.

NOTE: The facts provided for students in this unit provide a basis from which students can begin to make judgments about the relative effects of different technologies on the environment. However, the facts are inconclusive. No one yet knows enough about the long term effects of these technologies to make absolute judgments. One of the purposes of this unit is to help your students begin to see how difficult it is to evaluate the long term effects of technologies.

In Exercise I, your students will probably be frustrated by the lack of criteria with which to make an evaluation. Even with the additional information provided for Exercise III, your students may still experience some frustration with the lack of criteria and facts for making a judgment. As you will see on page 43, there are no "right" answers to this problem. When students raise concerns about their frustrations, help them to see the need both for clear criteria and more facts to solve this problem more adequately. Explain that such information is not yet available, and encourage them to continue to seek the information needed to make decisions about these technologies in the future.

UNIT V: MAKING JUDGMENTS
and
HOW DOES TECHNOLOGY AFFECT THE ENVIRONMENT?

INTRODUCTION

The appropriateness of a technology depends in part on how it affects the ENVIRONMENT in which it is used.

The ENVIRONMENT includes all of the land, water, and living things (plants, animals, people) in an area. In the desert, the environment includes sand, air, cacti, snakes, people, etc. On the coast of Iceland, the environment includes air, snow, ice, tundra, seals, fish, etc.

A technology is most appropriate when it does not hurt or change the environment.

EXERCISE I

Directions: Below are sketches of five houses. The houses are very much the same. Five people live in each, and each is designed and insulated in the same way. Each house is heated in a different way. The words under the drawings tell what form of energy technology is used to heat each house.

On the line provided below each house, rate each house as to how its energy use affects the environment. Use a scale of 1 to 10 to rate the houses. A rating of 1 means the house's heating system does little to hurt the environment. A rating of 10 means the system does great harm to the environment. Use the numbers 1 through 10 to show how much you think the energy use in each house affects the environment.

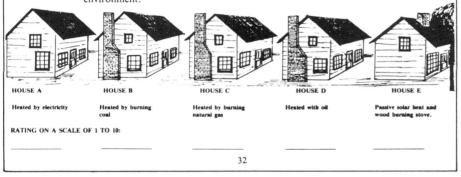

HOUSE A	HOUSE B	HOUSE C	HOUSE D	HOUSE E
Heated by electricity	Heated by burning coal	Heated by burning natural gas	Heated with oil	Passive solar heat and wood burning stove.

RATING ON A SCALE OF 1 TO 10:

_____   _____   _____   _____   _____

32

Suggested Directions for Unit V

1. Organize your class into groups of three or four.

2. Ask students to read the "Introduction" (page 32) to themselves. Discuss the concept of environment with students, giving other examples of different environments or asking students for examples.

Approximate time: 5 minutes

3. Have students read the directions for Exercise I (page 32). Clarify the rating system if it is unclear to students. Emphasize that each of the houses is to be rated individually, not in comparison with other houses.

Ask students to complete Exercise I in their groups. Because students are not yet given the specific criteria with which to make their judgments at this point in the unit, they may find this exercise frustrating. Do not give students more than 10 minutes to complete Exercise I.

After 10 minutes, ask one student from each group to report the group's ratings. Ask students on what basis they made their decisions, and what might have helped them make a better judgment about each house.

15 minutes

MAKING JUDGMENTS: FACT AND OPINION

How did you decide on a rating for each house in Exercise I? Did you have the information you needed to make a good decision?

Making good choices or judgments often depends on having the *facts*. Without facts, you may end up basing your choice on *opinion* only.

A *fact* is something (events, pieces of information, data) which is accepted as true.

An *opinion* is a person's idea or belief. People may have different opinions or interpretations of the same event, data, or experience.

Example: *Fact:* John has brown hair.
Opinion: John's hair is beautiful.

Fact: The sun will set at 7:02 p.m.
Opinion: My view of the sunset is better than yours.

EXERCISE II

Directions: Below are five sentences about strip mining for coal. Each sentence is either a fact or an opinion. In the space provided next to each sentence, write *fact* if you think it is a fact, or *opinion* if you think it is an opinion.

fact 1. Strip mining is the least expensive way to remove coal from the earth.

opinion 2. The least expensive way is always the best for everyone.

fact 3. In strip mining, soil and rock are stripped away so that the coal can be collected.

fact 4. It often takes thousands of years before dry areas that have been strip mined return to their natural condition.

opinion 5. Coal is the most valuable resource in the U.S. today.

MAKING JUDGMENTS: USING CRITERIA

Once you have found the facts which will help you make a judgment, you need a way of comparing them. It is useful to develop CRITERIA or standards against which you can judge your information.

Example: Below are 4 *criteria* useful in judging how different kinds of energy technology affect the environment.

1. The technology should have little immediate or long term effect on living things.

2. The technology should not make the environment smell or look unpleasant.

3. The environment should be able to recover quickly from the technology.

4. The technology should not produce a lot of waste material.

33

---

4. Have students read "Making Judgments: Fact And Opinion" (page 33) to themselves, or read it aloud. Go over the Example (page 33) with students. Ask students to generate other examples to indicate their understanding of the difference between facts and opinions.
   5-10 minutes

5. Have students read the directions to Exercise II (page 33) and complete the exercise in their groups. Have groups compare their responses. Discuss as necessary.
   5-10 minutes

6. Read "Making Judgments: Using Criteria" (page 33) aloud, or have a student read it aloud. Then, read the four criteria in the Example (page 33), and discuss these as standards by which different technologies can be judged.
   5-10 minutes

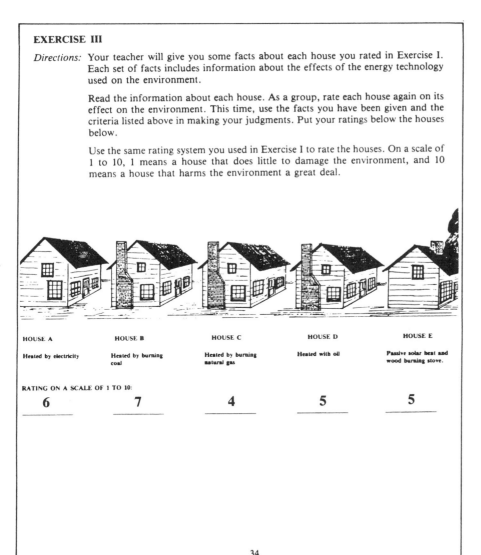

EXERCISE III

Directions: Your teacher will give you some facts about each house you rated in Exercise I. Each set of facts includes information about the effects of the energy technology used on the environment.

Read the information about each house. As a group, rate each house again on its effect on the environment. This time, use the facts you have been given and the criteria listed above in making your judgments. Put your ratings below the houses below.

Use the same rating system you used in Exercise I to rate the houses. On a scale of 1 to 10, 1 means a house that does little to damage the environment, and 10 means a house that harms the environment a great deal.

HOUSE A	HOUSE B	HOUSE C	HOUSE D	HOUSE E
Heated by electricity	Heated by burning coal	Heated by burning natural gas	Heated with oil	Passive solar heat and wood burning stove.

RATING ON A SCALE OF 1 TO 10:

6	7	4	5	5

34

NOTE: As explained in the Note on page 40, there are no "right" answers to this exercise. The answers given are suggested, based on the facts available but also on opinions. You may want to use these answers. Or, you may want to evaluate the five houses yourself, and use the rankings which you generate. With either option, what is important is that you help your students understand both the need to evaluate the environmental costs of technologies and the difficulties in doing such evaluation.

7. Ask students to read the directions to Exercise III (page 34). Distribute the information about the houses, found on the following pages, to the groups. You may want to give each group one copy of the information and ask them to share it. This promotes listening skills and group cooperation. Have extra copies to give to students after the exercise for later reference. Emphasize again that each house should be rated individually, not in comparison with the other houses.

Note that the information given about House A suggests that electricity could be produced by fossil fuel or nuclear fission. Students should base their judgment about House A on whichever form of production is prevalent in their area.

When students have completed Exercise III, ask a student from each group to present the group's ratings. Compare group results and discuss similarities and differences. Refer students back to the *facts* in the readings and the *criteria* in the Example on page 33 if they find wide discrepancies in their judgments.

Ask students if they needed still more information in order to make good judgments. Explain that such information is not yet available, and encourage students to be alert to further information about the effects of energy technologies on the environment.

20 minutes

43

HOUSE A

This house has electric resistance heating. It uses approximately 25,000 kilowatt-hours of electricity a year. At the house, it produces no pollution or waste. But electricity must be generated in some way. If coal, oil, and natural gas are used, the pollution and other harmful effects will be similar to those described for Houses B, C, and D.

If nuclear fission is used, there is a small amount of highly radioactive waste produced each year which must be stored away for hundreds or thousands of years. Otherwise, it could cause an increase in diseases such as cancer and leukemia. Permanent ways of getting rid of or storing the waste are being studied, but at present storage is usually at the power plant and considered "temporary."

The power plant (where the electricity is produced) gives off no carbon dioxide, no nitrogen, no particles. However, water used for cooling purposes is often returned to nearby rivers warmer than it was when it was taken out. The change in temperature affects the plants and animals in that part of the river.

HOUSE B

This house has an airtight coal burning furnace. It uses four tons of anthracite coal, which produces two or three times as many particles in the air as the wood used in House E. The coal also produces large quantities of sulfur oxides, which combine with water in the atmosphere to form sulfuric acid. This acid corrodes metal and stone surfaces. When it rains, the sulfur oxides and acids are washed into lakes and streams, increasing the acidity of the water. The effect of this increased acidity is not yet fully understood, but scientists believe it may damage the plant and animal life in these bodies of water. Small amounts of carbon monoxide are also produced by this coal burning furnace.

The mining of this coal, usually by underground methods rather than strip mining, can be dangerous to the miners. It can also lead to underground fires in abandoned mines and cause acid runoff into streams near the mine.

HOUSE C

This house has a gas furnace. It consumes 1,400 hundred cubic feet of natural gas each year, which produces little pollution where it is burned. (Natural gas is commonly sold in units of one hundred cubic feet.)

The production of natural gas creates several kinds of pollution. It damages vegetation in the environment and makes the air around the production plant unhealthy to breathe.

Natural gas is also highly flammable. Producing and shipping it create the risk of explosion and fire. Gas is shipped as liquified natural gas, and extreme care must be taken as it is unloaded to be sure that no leaks occur.

HOUSE D

This house is heated with oil. It consumes 1,000 gallons each year which produce small amounts of sulfur oxides and carbon dioxide when burned. Offshore drilling of oil and spills from tankers carrying this fuel pose danger to the plant and animal life of the oceans. The danger is not fully understood, but oil is absorbed into the bodies of marine animals and is known to cause cancer. In Arctic regions, an oil spill could blacken ice, causing it to melt more quickly. This could cause widespread climate changes.

HOUSE E

This house has the same amount of window glass as the other houses, but there are no windows on the north side. These windows have been moved to the south side of the house. This house has been positioned so that trees and bushes will not block the south side in the winter. This allows the house to make full use of the sun's energy. Leaves on the trees provide shade in the summer.

This house uses wood burned in an airtight stove to provide back-up heating. Two cords of wood are used during a typical heating season. This amount of wood requires the cutting of several trees and causes pollution in the form of particles of carbon and carbon monoxide. These particles may make the air difficult to breathe. They may also cause cancer. The particles wash out of the air when it rains, darkening snow and tree trunks. The carbon monoxide changes to carbon dioxide fairly quickly. Carbon dioxide contributes to the "greenhouse effect," which will be studied in later units. Many scientists predict that an increase in the carbon dioxide level of the atmosphere will raise the world's temperature and trigger worldwide climate changes.

UNIT V SUMMARY

MAKING JUDGMENTS

To make good decisions or judgments, you need to have *facts* so that your decision is not based on *opinion* alone.

A *fact* is something which is accepted as true. Data you gather in science are facts.

An *opinion* is a person's idea or belief. Once you have facts or data, you can make interpretations or form opinions.

You also need to have *criteria* which serve as standards against which you can judge the facts you gather. Facts give you the information you need. Criteria help you use the facts to make judgments or decisions.

APPROPRIATE TECHNOLOGY AND THE ENVIRONMENT

The *environment* is the land, water, and living things in a particular area. A technology is most appropriate when it does not hurt or change the environment.

Four criteria for judging whether or not a technology is appropriate in its effects on the environment are:

1. The technology has little short or long term effect on living things.

2. The technology does not make the environment smell or look unpleasant.

3. The environment can recover from the technology quickly.

4. The technology does not produce a lot of waste material.

8. Review the Unit V Summary (page 35) with students.

UNIT VI: WORKING WITH GRAPHS
and
HOW CAN WE USE ENERGY EFFICIENTLY?

STUDY SKILL

Graphs are often used in science to present a great deal of information in a simplified form. Like the data tables presented in Unit IV, graphs allow students to make comparisons and judge relationships among several different pieces of information. Graphs may be especially useful for students who tend to learn best in a visual or pictorial mode.

This unit introduces students to circle graphs, bar graphs, and line graphs as three ways of presenting information. Students are asked to read, interpret, and in some cases, construct graphs about efficient energy use. The additional suggestions at the end of this unit provide students with more practice in making graphs.

ENERGY, EFFICIENCY, AND TECHNOLOGY

This unit suggests that efficiency is another consideration in using energy and technology appropriately.

Students are first introduced to the concept of *entropy*. Entropy is a law of thermodynamics which states that all systems tend toward randomness and dissipation of energy. The form of entropy described in this unit occurs in the process of conversion from one form of energy to another. During this process, energy is dissipated and therefore wasted. If much energy is lost in the conversion process, the technology being used is not efficient.

Circle graphs are used to show students the relative energy losses involved in several methods of energy conversion, such as fossil fuels converted to electricity and oil converted to heat. Circle and bar graphs are used to indicate how different sectors in our society (residential, industrial, etc.) use energy. A line graph illustrates the amount of energy used by these sectors of society between 1950 and 1978.

NOTE ABOUT INFORMATION IN THIS UNIT

The Teacher's Guide to this unit contains extra information about the data used in Exercise III. This information can be shared with students before or after the exercise, if you feel it would be useful for them at that time.

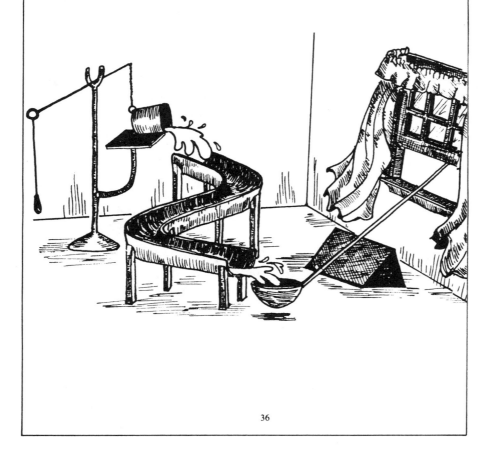

UNIT VI: WORKING WITH GRAPHS
and
HOW CAN WE USE ENERGY EFFICIENTLY?

INTRODUCTION

Look at the sketch below.

In the space provided on page 37, explain what you think this device does. Then list two things that are wrong with this device.

36

Suggested Directions for Unit VI

1. Organize your students into groups of three or four.

2. Ask students to read the "Introduction" (page 36). Have them identify what the device shown does and what is wrong with it. When students are done, ask several of them to share their answers with the class. Discuss how the device works and how energy, time, and water are wasted.

Approximate time: 10 minutes

48

This device ___opens the window_____

_____

Two things wrong with this device are:

1)___it wastes time, energy and water_____

_____

2)_____

_____

ENTROPY AND EFFICIENCY

In the E-Z Window Opener in the Introduction, human energy from someone's arm is turned into mechanical energy to open the window. But some of the energy used to pull down the short lever had to be used to lift the side of the bucket. Some energy was used to overcome friction, or the resistance that occurs when two objects rub together. This energy did nothing to open the window. It was turned into heat, and did no work. This loss of energy as it changes from one form to another is an example of ENTROPY.

It is impossible to convert energy from one form to another or transfer it from one place to another without losing some. But some technologies waste more energy than others. If much entropy occurs, the process used to convert energy is not EFFICIENT.

This unit will show you how information about energy efficiency can help you decide whether or not a technology is appropriate.

EXERCISE I

Directions: The picture on the next page represents a common way to burn oil to produce electricity. The electricity is then used to heat water. Entropy occurs here, just as it did in the E-Z Window Opener.

The paragraphs below the picture describe what happens in the picture. Read the paragraphs. Each time you come to a number in parentheses ( ) in the paragraphs, write that number in the appropriate place in the picture. Each number shows where entropy is taking place.

When you are done, answer the question below the paragraphs on page 38.

3. Read "Entropy And Efficiency" (page 37) aloud, or have a student read it aloud. Discuss with students the meanings of *entropy, efficient, friction,* and *converted.*

Ask students to read the directions for Exercise I (page 37) and to complete the exercise in their groups. When they have finished, discuss their responses to the question (page 38) of how to avoid entropy in the conversion of oil to hot water.

10–15 minutes

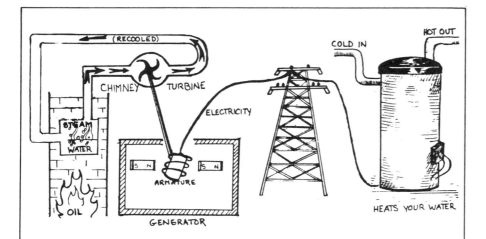

OIL TO ELECTRICITY TO HOT WATER

Three gallons of oil must be burned at the power plant to deliver the energy of one gallon of oil to your house. Two-thirds of the energy in the oil is lost when it is converted to electricity and transported to your house.

When oil is burned, only a part of the heat goes into the water at the power plant. Much of the heat goes up the chimney (1), and some goes to heat the container holding the water (2). As the water changes to steam, some of its heat is used to heat the pipes it passes through (3). When the steam turns the turbine, it must overcome friction (4). Energy is also used to overcome friction as it turns the armature (5). As the electricity created in the generator travels through wires from the power plant to your house, some of the electricity escapes from the wires into the air (6). Some heats the wires (7). At your house, most electricity you receive is used to heat the water.

Each check represents entropy. Explain one way you might be able to avoid energy loss in the process shown above.

Student answers will vary. Accept any reasonable answer. Note that no matter what techniques are used to maximize efficiency in this system, it is still only about 33% efficient. The best way to minimize entropy in this case is to burn the oil in the home to heat the water.

38

GRAPHS

As you may have already discovered, science often uses numbers as a way of explaining important ideas. In order to compare the numbers, they are sometimes organized into GRAPHS. As you found out in Unit V, you can become a better decision maker by comparing facts.

There are several different kinds of graphs. This unit will show you how to read and use CIRCLE GRAPHS, BAR GRAPHS, and LINE GRAPHS about energy efficiency.

CIRCLE GRAPHS

Circle graphs, or pie charts, are one way of presenting information so you can see it at a glance.

Each circle graph equals all, or 100%, of whatever it is showing. The circle can be divided to show parts, or percentages of the whole amount.

Example: This circle graph shows what portion of the oil burned in the power plant is actually used to heat water in your home.

67% lost   33% used

- The whole circle, 100%, is the amount of energy the power plant starts with.
- The shaded area represents the portion or percentage of the energy lost in the process.
- The unshaded area shows the portion or percentage of the oil actually used to heat your water at home.

39

4. Have students read "Graphs" and "Circle Graphs" (page 39). Go over the Example on page 39 for clarity.
   3–5 minutes

EXERCISE II

Directions: Below are circle graphs which show how much energy is actually used and how much is lost in five different technologies.

    1) Shade the "energy loss" section of each graph.

    2) Write in the percentage of energy loss on each graph.

    3) Answer the questions on the next page which ask you to compare the technologies shown in the graphs.

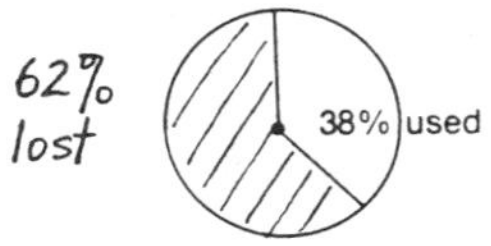

62% lost   38% used

Average fossil fuel converted to electricity

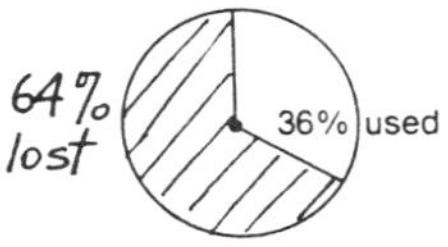

64% lost   36% used

Oil (converted to heat) burned in a fairly efficient furnace

55% lost   45% used

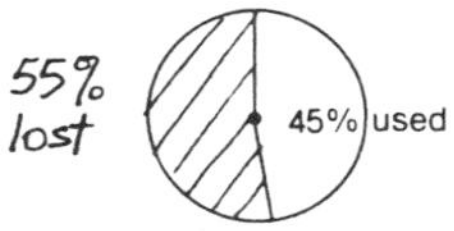

Steam engine (water converted to mechanical energy)

9% used   91% lost

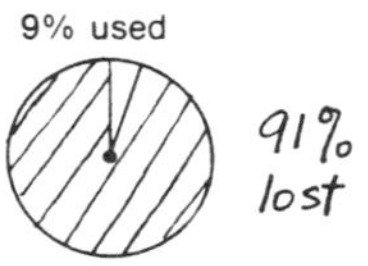

Gasoline burned in an automobile (gas converted to mechanical energy)

56% lost   44% used

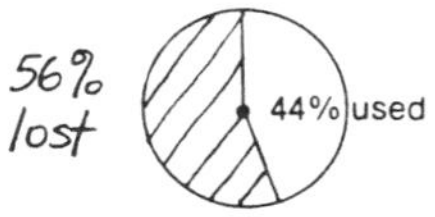

Natural gas converted to heat in a fairly efficient furnace

40

5. Ask students to read the directions for Exercise II (page 40) and to complete it in their groups. Go over the answers they have written for the questions on page 41. Point out that every conversion process involves entropy, but that some processes are more efficient than others. Discuss what students can do to become more efficient energy users.

15 minutes

QUESTIONS

1. How much energy is actually used when oil is converted to heat? ___36%___

2. How much energy is lost when natural gas is converted to heat? ___56%___

3. Which energy technology shown on page 40 is the most efficient (wastes the least energy)?
   ___steam engine___

4. Which two technologies are the least efficient? ___gasoline burned in___
   ___automobile and oil burned in furnace___

5. Explain one way you could cut down on your use of one of the least efficient energy
   technologies shown on page 40. ___Student answers will vary___
   _____
   _____
   _____

EXERCISE III

Directions: Below is some information about the amount of energy used and lost by different
sectors of society in the U.S.

Using the circle next to each set of information, make a circle graph that shows
energy used and lost in each area of society. Then, shade in the section of each
graph that shows how much energy is lost.

1. Residential (home) energy use: 76% used   1.
   24% lost

2. Commercial energy use (stores,   76% used   2.
   restaurants, schools):   24% lost

3. Industrial energy use: 60% used   3.
   40% lost

4. Transportation energy use: 22% used   4.
   78% lost

5. Generation of electricity: 33% used   5.
   67% lost

41

The *residential sector* uses energy to heat space and water, to run appliances such as stereos, lamps, and dishwashers, to pump water for wells and swimming pools, etc. It uses the following percentages of these fuels:

Natural gas 39.5%
Fuel oil and kerosene .. 21.6%
Propane, butane, etc. .. 5.9%
Electricity 32.9%

(From *Patterns of Energy Consumption in the U.S.,* Office of Science and Technology, Executive Office of the President, Washington, D.C., 1972. Note that these percentages have not changed significantly since 1972.)

The *commercial sector* uses energy to heat space and water and to run lights and appliances.

The *industrial sector* uses energy for a variety of manufacturing processes, such as fabricating plastic, synthesizing chemicals, producing glass, smelting copper, producing steel, etc.

The *transportation sector* uses energy primarily in the automobile, but it also includes trucks, buses, ships, diesel driven trains, trolley cars, etc.

The *generation of electricity* can be from coal, oil, natural gas, hydroelectric power, geothermal power, or nuclear fission. In 1982, the percentages of each used to generate electricity were:

Coal 53.2%
Hydropower 13.8%
Natural gas 13.6%
Nuclear 12.6%
Petroleum 6.5%

(From National Energy Information Center, Department of Energy.)

6. Have students read the directions for and complete Exercise III (page 41) in their groups. Again, discuss with students ways in which they might reduce their energy use in those sectors in which they have a role, i.e., residential, commercial, and transportation.

10 minutes

BAR GRAPHS

Each circle graph shows you one set of information at a time. With a BAR GRAPH you can compare several different pieces of information according to the same standard.

In a BAR GRAPH the standard is presented along the left hand side of the paper. The pieces of information are shown along the bottom. Each bar shows where along the standard the information falls.

Example: The bar graph below shows some of the same information presented on the circle graphs in Exercise III, page 41. It shows the percentage of energy lost in each sector of society. The bar graph lets you compare the efficiency of energy use of the different sectors.

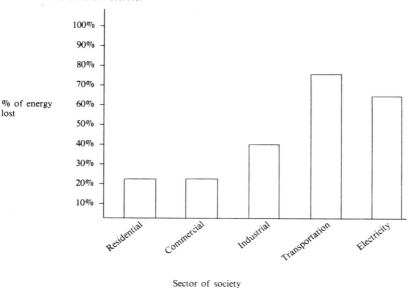

- The left side of the graph is divided into percentages of energy lost. This is the standard.

- The bottom of the graph shows each sector of society that uses energy.

- Each bar shows the percentage of energy lost in each sector of society.

42

7. Ask students to read "Bar Graphs" (page 42). Work through the Example on page 42 with your students, clarifying what each part of the bar graph represents.

5–10 minutes

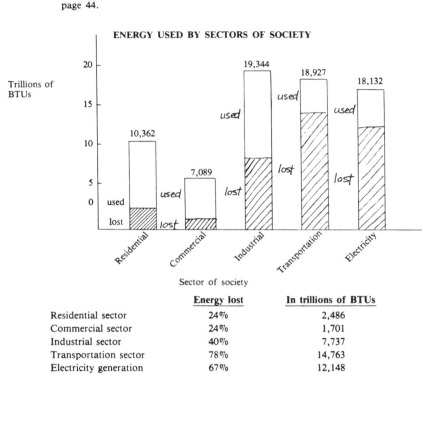
8. Have students read the directions to Exercise IV (page 43). You may want to go over the bar graph for Exercise IV with students before they begin the exercise so that it is clear to them. When students have finished, discuss the responses they have given to the questions and the implications of the information on the graph for their own energy use and choices.

15 minutes

QUESTIONS

1. Which sector of society uses the most energy? ___*industrial*___
2. Which sector of society uses the least energy? ___*transportation*___
3. Which two sectors of society are least efficient in their energy use? ___*transportation*___
    ___*electricity*___
4. Which two sectors of society use energy most efficiently? ___*residential*___
    ___*commercial*___

LINE GRAPHS

A third type of graph is a LINE GRAPH. A line graph is built on two sets of information, one presented along the left side or *vertical axis* of the graph, and one shown along the bottom or *horizontal axis* of the graph. Each point on the graph shows you two pieces of information.

By connecting related points on a line graph, you can see how the information changes over time or is related to other information.

Example: The line graph below shows the amount of energy used in the residential and commercial sectors of society in the U.S. between 1950 and 1978. The graph is explained on the next page. Look at the graph as you read through this explanation.

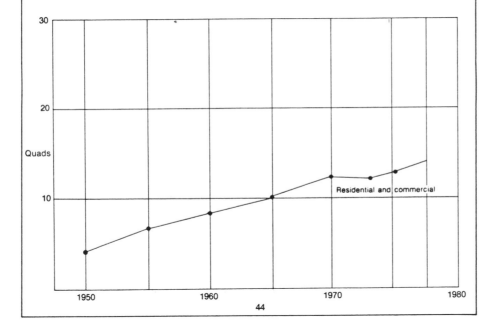

44

9. Have students read "Line Graphs" (page 44). Go over the line graph presented in the Example on page 44 and the explanation of the example given on page 45. Be sure students can locate and read the horizontal and vertical axes of the graph. Ask students questions about the graph to be sure they understand how to use it. For example: How much energy did the residential and commercial sectors use in 1970?

10 minutes

Explanation

- The left side (vertical axis) of the graph shows energy use in quads. A quad equals one quadrillion BTUs.

- The bottom line (horizontal axis) of the graph shows the years between 1950 and 1978.

- The line on the graph shows the change in the number of quads of energy used in the residential and commercial sectors between 1950 and 1978.

To find out how much energy the residential and commercial sectors of society used in any one year, find that year on the horizontal axis of the graph. Use a straight edge to find the place on the line directly above the year on the horizontal axis. Mark that point. Then, use a straight edge to find the point on the vertical axis directly to the left of the point you have marked on the line. That number on the vertical axis is the number of quads of energy used in the residential and commercial sectors in the year you are looking at.

For example, in 1960, the residential and commercial sectors used about 8 quads of energy.

EXERCISE V

Directions: The graph below is similar to the graph in the *Example* on page 44, except that it shows energy use in four different sectors of society: residential and commercial, industrial, transportation, and electricity.

Look over the graph to see what it tells you. Then, use the graph to help you answer the questions on page 46.

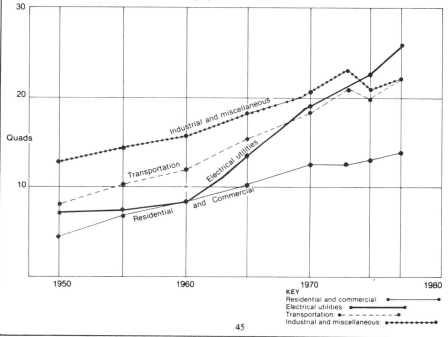

KEY
Residential and commercial: ●━━━━━●
Electrical utilities: ●━━━━●
Transportation: ●━ ━ ━ ━ ━ ●
Industrial and miscellaneous: ●●●●●●●●●●

45

10. Ask students to read the directions for Exercise V (page 45) and to complete the exercise in their groups. When they are done, discuss the answers they gave to the questions on page 46.
15–20 minutes

QUESTIONS

1. Which sector used the most energy in 1978? _electrical utilities_

2. Which sector used the least energy in 1978? _residential and commercial_

3. About how many quads of energy did the transportation sector of society use in 1970? ___
   17 quads

4. Which sector of society had the biggest increase in energy use between 1960 and 1978? (Subtract the number of quads of energy used in 1960 from the number used in 1978. The sector in which the number is biggest increased its energy use the most.)
   electrical utilities

5. Explain one thing the U.S. might do to decrease its energy use in the sector of society which uses the most energy.
   Students' answers will vary. Possible answers may include turning off lights when not in use, switching to solar energy.

UNIT VI SUMMARY

GRAPHS

Graphs are pictures which let you see a lot of information at once. Graphs also help you compare pieces of information so you can make decisions or judgments about them.

CIRCLE GRAPHS are circles divided into parts.

38% energy used   62% energy lost

BAR GRAPHS put information into a form that lets you compare.

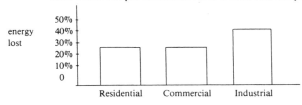

energy lost

50%
40%
30%
20%
10%
0

Residential   Commercial   Industrial

Sector of society

LINE GRAPHS present the changes in information over time.

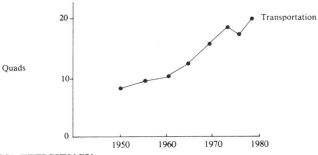

Quads

20

10

0

1950   1960   1970   1980

Transportation

ENERGY EFFICIENCY

Efficiency is an important consideration in judging the appropriateness of a technology and choosing which technology is appropriate.

When converting energy from one form to another, energy is often lost through ENTROPY. Energy use is most efficient where the least entropy occurs.

All sectors of society have some entropy. The most entropy occurs in the transportation and electrical generation sectors. It is in these sectors especially that we must develop more efficient energy use.

47

11. Review the Unit VI Summary (page 47) with students.

UNIT VII: SOLVING PROBLEMS
and
HOW MUCH DO TECHNOLOGIES COST?

STUDY SKILLS

Most scientific disciplines require students to solve problems. We ask students to begin with a question or problem and to generate an answer or solution. But most students lack systematic ways of approaching and dealing with the problems they encounter. They tend to depend on a trial and error method and to "freeze" when their usual approach is ineffective.

This unit leads students through a five-step problem solving strategy. Each step in the sequence is a skill in itself; together the steps provide students with one way of solving problems in science and in their daily lives. The five steps are presented below.

1. POSING THE QUESTION: In this step, students analyze a situation and define the precise nature of the problem in the form of a question.

2. SELECTING DATA: In step two, students identify information needed to solve the problem and plan how to get it.

3. GATHERING DATA: In this step, students carry out their plans to collect information needed to solve the problem.

4. ORGANIZING DATA: In step four, students organize the information they have gathered, possibly into tables or graphs. Organizing the data allows students to see patterns that can help them answer their questions.

5. DRAWING CONCLUSIONS: In this step, students examine the organized data and try to come up with an answer to their question or a solution to the problem posed in Step One.

Unit VII takes students through these five steps. If you find students lacking in one or more of the skills which comprise the sequence, you may want to create additional opportunities for them to practice these skills.

A NOTE ABOUT LEARNING STYLE

The strategy presented in this unit is a linear one, consisting of a logical sequence of processes. There are two important qualifications to keep in mind and to share with students when working on this unit.

1. Different problems may require different problem solving strategies. No one problem solving strategy will automatically equip students to solve any and all problems they may confront. Ideally, students will eventually learn several strategies and develop the skill of selecting an appropriate strategy from a number of alternatives.

2. Not all students will be comfortable with or perform well using a linear, logical strategy such as the one presented in this unit, although it is still a valuable process for them to learn. Some students can come up with a solution to a problem but are unable to explain how they derived it. Others may simply "know" the answer through some kind of intuition. Still others may be adept at solving visual problems but be at a loss in approaching problems stated in words.

There should be room in the science classroom for the student whose problem solving strategies are non-linear. Any strategy for solving problems which produces accurate results is worthy of recognition. A goal in science teaching is to make students aware of several alternative problem solving strategies from which they can choose the one best for themselves and most appropriate to the situation. This unit presents one such strategy.

LIFE CYCLE COST ANALYSIS AND APPROPRIATE TECHNOLOGY

Life cycle cost analysis takes into consideration not only the initial cost of an item but also the cost of using, maintaining, and ultimately replacing it. Products which are durable and reliable are favored by life cycle cost analysis because they tend to have lower maintenance costs and last longer, even though they may cost more initially.

Technologies are more appropriate when they use materials which are *durable,* i.e., expected to last a long time, and *reliable,* i.e., have a minimal need for maintenance and repair. There is often a direct relationship between the durability of a technology and its degree of complexity. Because less complex products and machines have fewer moving parts, they tend to last longer than more complex technologies.

The bicycle, the example used in this unit, is itself an appropriate technology for traveling short distances. The unit takes this observation one step further and asks whether some bicycles are more appropriate than others. Students are presented with a variety of data about two different bicycles and are asked to organize it in a way that permits them to draw a conclusion about the appropriateness of each. Criteria for judging appropriateness include first cost, life cycle cost, durability, and reliability.

UNIT VII: SOLVING PROBLEMS
and
HOW MUCH DO TECHNOLOGIES COST?

INTRODUCTION

Your teacher will ask three of you to read the conversation below aloud. As you listen and follow along, think about what Lisa's problem is and how she might go about solving it. After the conversation has been read, write your ideas in the space provided.

LISA'S PROBLEM

Mother: Lisa, the local newspaper called today to say that your application for a weekend paper route has been approved.

Lisa: Oh, thank goodness! I thought they'd never get around to calling me. How soon do I have to let them know I want it?

Mother: By next Monday.

Lisa: That's no problem.

Mother: Well, I don't know. How do you plan to deliver all those papers every weekend? You know I won't be able to drive you around the neighborhood in the car, and it's too much walking with all that weight.

Lisa: I've got that all figured out, Mom. I can take some money out of my savings account and buy a new bicycle with it.

Father: Now hold on! You're supposed to be saving that money for college.

Lisa: Oh, Dad! I can replace it out of the money I earn from the paper route, plus put in a whole lot more.

Mother: Just how much do you plan on spending for this bicycle?

Lisa: Well, there's this great ten speed on sale down at the Bike Hut for only $140.

Mother: Oh, Lisa! That's way too much money to spend on just a bicycle!

Lisa: Come on, Mother! It's a great bike!

Father: Wait a minute. Lisa, how much did the paper say you would earn if you take the route?

Lisa: Almost $3 a week. I know it's not that much at first, but it goes up each year. Howie Larsen's already making $4 a week and its only his third year.

Father: Well, let's see. That makes $156 the first year. If you add on the cost of a bicycle license and normal maintenance, it will take over a year to earn back all the money you want to take out of your savings account. And that doesn't count the interest you would earn if you left the money in the bank.

Mother: Why don't you find a used bicycle for less money? That way you'd make a profit in the first year.

48

Suggested Directions for Unit VII

1. Organize your class into groups of three or four.

2. Have students read the "Introduction" (page 48). Ask three students to read the conversation between Lisa and her parents aloud for the whole class. Have students answer the questions found after the conversation. When students have finished, ask several of them to explain what they think Lisa's problem is and how she should try to solve it. Encourage them to think of problem solving in terms of a sequence of events. Keep track of their ideas on the board. At this point, accept all student answers as possible approaches to the problem.

Approximate time: 10 minutes

3. Have students read "Problem Solving" (page 49). Explain that this unit will present one problem solving approach that will be useful in science and in their own lives but that other ways of solving problems may also be useful to them.

5 minutes

STEP ONE: POSING THE QUESTION

In the first step in problem solving, you have to take aim on the problem, just like a sharpshooter takes aim on the target before firing. You must know *exactly* what question you are trying to answer *right from the start,* or you may waste valuable time.

The first step in solving a problem, then, is to ask yourself, "What exactly do I want to find out?"

EXERCISE I

Directions: Re-read the conversation on pages 48–49 between Lisa and her parents. Then, work with your group to decide exactly what Lisa's problem is. Write the problem in the form of a question on the lines below.

Answers will vary. See Suggested Direction below for guidelines.

LIFE CYCLE COST

In Unit V, you learned that it was useful to have criteria in making judgments. Criteria are also useful in helping to solve problems. In solving Lisa's problem, a key criterion is the life cycle cost of the bicycle she will buy.

When you go to buy a product or a piece of machinery, you usually look at how much it costs before you buy it. That is the product's *first cost.* But you also need to think about other hidden costs before you make your decision.

The *life cycle cost* of the product or machine is how much it will cost during the time that you own and use it. This includes whatever it costs to *buy* it, to *use* it, to *maintain* it or keep it running, and eventually to *replace* it when it wears out.

The life cycle cost of a product or machine will be lowest if the product is:

> *durable* — it will last a long time, *and*
>
> *reliable* — it doesn't need much maintenance or repair.

A technology is more appropriate if its life cycle cost is low, that is, if it is durable and reliable. Lisa needs to find out which bicycle will have the lower life cycle cost so that she can answer her question.

50

4. Read "Step One: Posing the Question" (page 50) aloud, or have a student read it aloud.
   5 minutes

5. Have students read the directions to Exercise I (page 50) and complete it in their groups. When they are done, ask one student from each group to write the group's question on the board. Help students select one question to serve as the basis for the rest of this unit. If none of the questions will serve, help them write another question, drawing on as many ideas from the group-generated questions as possible.

   No one question works best in this unit. We suggest, however, that the question you choose addresses Lisa's parents' concern that the money she withdraws from her savings account to buy the bicycle be replaced as soon as possible. One possible question is:

   > Which bicycle — new or used — will pay for itself faster?

   Groups may generate questions such as:

   > Which bike is best for Lisa to buy?
   > Which bike is the better buy?

   Students need to understand that such vague questions will make their search for an answer difficult. The question must include some criteria for judging the relative merits of each bike so that students can identify the information they will need to draw a conclusion. Stating the question clearly is crucial for effective problem solving.
   10 minutes

6. Have students read "Life Cycle Cost" (page 50), or read it aloud. Be sure that students understand the terms *first cost, life cycle cost, durable,* and *reliable.* Ask students for examples from their own experience that illustrate these terms. Point out that this section provides students with specific criteria, or ways of judging, which will help them solve Lisa's problem.
   5–10 minutes

STEP TWO: SELECTING DATA

Now that you know what the problem is and have stated it in the form of a question, you are ready for the next step.

If you had to travel all the way across town to a friend's house where you had never been before, you would need information in order to get there. You would need to know names of streets, turns to make, and distances to travel.

Problem solving is similar. There are certain pieces of information, or DATA, which you need to answer the question posed in Step One. In Step Two, SELECTING DATA, you identify the pieces of information you need and decide where to look for them.

EXERCISE II

Directions: Working with your group, list the pieces of information Lisa needs to answer the question your class has posed for her. Next to each piece of information on the list, write where you think Lisa can get that information. Use the space below to make your lists. Keep in mind the life cycle costs (use, maintenance, replacement) described above.

INFORMATION NEEDED

Possible answers:

- What she can expect to earn per week from her paper route.

- Amount of interest she will not earn if she withdraws money to purchase each bicycle.

WHERE TO GET IT

Local newspaper

Bank

51

7. Read "Step Two: Selecting Data" (page 51) aloud, or have a student read it aloud. Discuss as necessary. Ask students to read the directions to Exercise II (page 51) and complete the exercise in their groups. When they are done, have each group read its lists. Make a class list on the board of all the ideas. Have students eliminate unnecessary or irrelevant information for answering the question posed in Exercise I, and add any information that is missing. Have students add or delete items from their own lists so that each student has a complete list of the information needed.

15 minutes

STEP THREE: GATHERING DATA

Once you know what it is you are trying to find out (POSING THE QUESTION) and what pieces of information you need in order to come up with an answer (SELECTING DATA) you are ready for Step Three: GATHERING DATA.

GATHERING DATA means collecting the information you need and writing it down clearly and neatly so you can read and use it later. You don't need to figure out the answer to your problem yet. Just collect and record the pieces of information you need.

EXERCISE III

Directions: Read the conversations below with your group. Then, go back through each conversation and write down the information given which you will need to answer Lisa's question. Use the space provided after the conversations to write down your information. Be sure all information is clearly labeled.

Use the list you wrote on page 51 to help you keep track of information you need.

LISA GATHERS INFORMATION

Scene: The Bike Hut

Lisa: Excuse me, can you help me please?

Salesperson: I'll try. What are you looking for?

Lisa: Well, actually I need some information. Is that blue ten speed in the window still on sale?

Sales: Yes. It will sell for $140 through next Friday. Then it goes back up to $175. Are you thinking of buying it?

Lisa: I'm not sure yet. Can you give me some idea of how much I'd have to spend in order to keep it in good shape and the cost of a license and things like that?

Sales: You mean the life cycle cost?

Lisa: What's that?

Sales: The cost of buying, using, maintaining, and eventually replacing your bicycle.

Lisa: Yes, I guess I need to know the life cycle cost.

Sales: Okay. To begin with, a bicycle license costs $15 no matter what bike you buy.

Lisa: Will I have to buy a new one each year?

Sales: No, just once. As far as maintenance goes, it's not bad at all. It will vary from year to year, but if you take good care of it, you shouldn't have to spend more than $15 a year to keep it in working order.

Lisa: That's great! How long do you think it would last before I'd have to replace it?

Sales: Oh, ten years at least. Now, were you thinking about getting some insurance?

Lisa: No, why?

52

8. Have students read "Step Three: Gathering Data" (page 52). Ask them to read the directions for Exercise III (page 52) and complete the exercise in their groups. Discuss each group's findings as a class to be sure that all students have identified the information they will need.
15–20 minutes

Sales: A lot of ten speeds have been stolen around town lately. You can insure the bike you're interested in for only $5 a year. That way, if it's stolen, you'll have enough money to replace it.

Lisa: I think I've got all that down. Now, my mother wants me to find out about a used bike, too. Just in case the ten speed is too much.

Sales: We have a pretty good one in the back for only $55, but I don't think it will last more than three years.

Lisa: How much do you think I would have to spend a year to keep that one going?

Sales: Probably around $45. But you'd have to rent a replacement bike while the used one was in the shop being fixed. That would cost around $15 a year.

Lisa: A used bike sure doesn't sound like a good idea.

Sales: Well, it all depends on what you plan to use it for.

Lisa: A paper route.

Sales: Well, that would certainly wear it out fast. You'd end up having to replace it after three years. By then, a ten speed bike like the one in the window will probably cost around $200.

Lisa: Well, that tells me all I need to know. I'll let you know what I decide. Thanks for your help.

Sales: You're welcome. Good luck!

Scene: The local newspaper office

Editor: What can I do for you, Miss?

Lisa: I'm trying to find out how much I'll make a week if I take the weekend paper route your paper has offered me.

Editor: That's easy. $3 a week your first year, $3.50 your second, $4 your third, and $4.50 your fourth. Keeps going up 50 cents a year.

Lisa: That's it?

Editor: Yep, except for tips from your customers, but you shouldn't count on that.

Lisa: Okay. Thanks a lot.

Editor: Any time.

* * * * * * * * *

Scene: Lisa's bank

Lisa: Can you tell me how much interest I would lose in a year if I withdrew $140 from my savings account?

Teller: Yes, that comes to $7.

Lisa: How about if I only withdrew $55?

Teller: Then you would only lose $2.75 interest.

Lisa: Thank you very much.

* * * * * * * * *

53

INFORMATION GATHERED FROM LISA'S CONVERSATIONS:

STEP FOUR: ORGANIZING DATA

Now that you have gathered your data, you may be tempted to jump right in and start drawing conclusions. Beware! Unless you have organized your data, you may be wasting your time.

The fourth step in problem solving is ORGANIZING DATA by putting it into a chart or graph that helps you make sense out of it. Organizing the information often shows you patterns or ideas which will lead you to the answer you are looking for.

Example: Below is a data table which organizes the information Lisa gathered about the two bicycles at the Bike Hut.

Data Table #1

COST OF BICYCLES

	Used Bicycle	New Bicycle
Useful life	3 years	10 years
Purchase price	$ 55	$140
Unearned interest (on money withdrawn from bank)	$ 2.75	$ 7
License	$ 15	$ 15
Insurance (each year)	0	$ 5
Maintenance (each year)	$ 45	$ 15
Rental bike during repair	$ 15	0
Replacement cost after 4 years	$200 (for a new bicycle)	0
TOTAL COST after 1 year	$132.75	$182
TOTAL COST after 2 years	$195.50	$209
TOTAL COST after 3 years	$258.25	$236
TOTAL COST after 4 years	$506	$263

54

9. Read "Step Four: Organizing Data" (page 54) aloud, or have a student read it aloud. Go over the data table, "Cost of Bicycles" given in the Example (page 54). Be sure that students understand the TOTAL COST for each year at the bottom of the data table, since they will need to use that information in Exercise IV.

Please note: In Data Table #1, unearned interest on money withdrawn from savings is calculated at a rate of 5%. For the sake of clarity in the problem, the interest is not compounded but remains constant over the four years. In computing the fourth year cost for the used bicycle, be sure to include the unearned interest from the money used to purchase the used bike ($2.75) and from the $200 used to buy the replacement bike ($10).

Directions: Below and on page 56 are two more data tables to help you organize the data you have gathered about Lisa's problem. The data table "EARNINGS FROM WEEKEND NEWSPAPER ROUTE" has been completed for you.

Use Data Table #1 in the *Example* on page 54 and Data Table #2 below to complete Data Table on the next page: "PROFIT FROM NEWSPAPER ROUTE." You will find the information you need about *cost* in Data Table #1 and the information about *earnings* in Data Table #2.

Data Table #2

EARNINGS FROM WEEKEND NEWSPAPER ROUTE

Year	Weekly Pay	Yearly Pay	Cumulative Pay*
1	$3.00	$156	$156
2	$3.50	$182	$338
3	$4.00	$208	$546
4	$4.50	$234	$780

*Cumulative pay is the total amount Lisa has earned at the end of each year. It includes all the money she has earned that year *plus* all her earnings from the year(s) before.

Lisa's Data Table #3

Use information from the data tables on page 54 and above to complete the data table on the next page, "PROFIT FROM NEWSPAPER ROUTE."

Costs come from the total costs at the bottom of Data Table #1, "COST OF BICYCLES."

Earnings come from the Cumulative Pay column of Data Table #2, "EARNINGS FROM WEEKEND NEWSPAPER ROUTE."

Profit = Earnings minus Costs.

10. Have students read the directions for Exercise IV (page 55). Before they begin working on the exercise, discuss the information given to them in the data table, "Earnings From Weekend Newspaper Route" (page 55). Also, be sure that students are clear about what information the third data table, "Profit From Newspaper Route" (page 56) requires. Have students work in their groups to complete Exercise IV. When they are done, have groups compare their data tables to be sure that they have completed them correctly.

20 minutes

PROFIT FROM NEWSPAPER ROUTE

Time	Item	Used Bicycle	New Bicycle
End of 1st year	Earnings	$156	$156
	Cost	$132.75	$182
	Profit	$23.25	$ -26
End of 2nd year	Earnings	$338	$338
	Cost	$195.50	$209
	Profit	$142.50	$129
End of 3rd year	Earnings	$546	$546
	Cost	$258.25	$236
	Profit	$287.75	$310
End of 4th year	Earnings	$780	$780
	Cost	$506	$263
	Profit	$274	$517

STEP FIVE: DRAWING CONCLUSIONS

So far, in solving Lisa's problem, you have

POSED THE QUESTION,

SELECTED DATA you needed to answer the question,

GATHERED DATA needed to answer the question, and

ORGANIZED DATA in a way that allows possible patterns in the data to catch your eye.

Perhaps you have already noticed a pattern within the data you have organized. The word *pattern* suggests repetition, like the pattern on wallpaper. The same picture or idea keeps reappearing as you look at it.

Data can repeat itself in the same way. As you look at the data you have collected and organized, try to find facts that fit together to form a pattern or a complete picture.

To DRAW A CONCLUSION or solve your problem, ask yourself the same question you posed back in Step One. Then, look for the patterns in your organized data. If an answer to your question exists, that's where you are most likely to find it.

56

11. Read "Step Five: Drawing Conclusions" (page 56) aloud, or have a student read it aloud. Discuss as necessary.

3–5 minutes

Directions: Turn back to page 56, and examine Lisa's third data table. Look for patterns in the data which will help you answer the question you posed in Step One.

Write your answer to that question and your reasons for choosing that answer on the lines below. Keep in mind the ideas of *first cost, life cycle cost, durability,* and *reliability* in making your decision.

Answer to question posed in Step One (on page 50): _____

See discussion in Suggested Direction 12 below.

_____

_____

_____

Reasons for choosing that answer: _____

_____

_____

_____

LISA CHOOSES A BICYCLE

Father: Well, Lisa, what did you find out?

Lisa: To begin with, Mom was right about that used bike. It would pay for itself faster than the new one.

Mother: I had a feeling it would.

Father: I guess that settles it.

Lisa: I don't think so, Dad.

Father: Why not?

Lisa: Because I also found out that the new bike will allow me to make more money in the long run. Look at this data table and I'll show you what I mean.

Mother: Yes, I do see what you mean. I guess it just goes to show that durability can be just as important as how much something costs.

Lisa: What do you think, Dad?

Father: I think you better hurry down to the Bike Hut and buy that new ten speed before the sale ends!

57

---

12. Ask students to read the directions for Exercise V (page 57) and complete it in their groups. Have each group read its conclusion, and then discuss the groups' reasons for their conclusions.

These questions may help focus the discussion:

Why is the more expensive new bicycle actually more profitable over the long run?

What are some of the hidden costs in buying the used bicycle?

Which bicycle is more durable? More reliable?

Which bicycle will provide Lisa with the more appropriate form of transportation?

A number of possible conclusions can be drawn from the data in table #3, "Profits From Weekend Newspaper Route," but there is only one answer to the question, "Which bicycle will pay for itself faster?" The data shows that the used bicycle pays back its cost during the first year of Lisa's paper route, leaving her with $23.25 profit the first year and $142.50 profit the second year. The new bicycle only pays back $129 in profits after two years. The used bicycle pays for itself faster.

Your students should notice that the new bicycle becomes the more profitable purchase sometime during the third year of the paper route, and that in the fourth year, the purchase of a new bicycle to replace the worn out used one actually results in a significant loss in profit.

10 minutes

13. Have three students read the parts in "Lisa Chooses A Bicycle" (page 57) aloud while the rest of the class follows in their text. Discuss Lisa's decision.

5 minutes

71

UNIT VII SUMMARY

PROBLEM SOLVING

Solving problems is easier when you have a plan or set of directions that helps you get from the problem to an answer. One possible plan is to follow these five steps:

1) POSE THE QUESTION: Figure out exactly what the problem is and put it into question form.

2) SELECT THE DATA: Decide what pieces of information or data you need to solve the problem and where you can find them.

3) GATHER DATA: Find and write down the information you need to solve the problem or answer the question.

4) ORGANIZE DATA: Use data tables, graphs, or charts to help you put the information together so you can see patterns in the data.

5) DRAW CONCLUSIONS: Look for patterns in your organized data, and answer the question you posed in Step One.

APPROPRIATE TECHNOLOGY – LIFE CYCLE COSTS

So far, we have seen that technologies are more appropriate when they:

- use local resources
- are community operated
- use renewable energy
- have little effect on the environment
- use energy efficiently.

Life cycle cost must be considered when choosing an appropriate technology. The life cycle cost includes the first cost of the technology as well as the cost over time to use, repair, and replace.

A technology is more appropriate if it is durable and reliable over time. It is durable if it lasts a long time, and it is reliable if it does not need much maintenance or repair.

58

14. Review the Unit VII Summary (page 58) with students.

UNIT VIII: BECOMING A SKILLED TEST TAKER
and
APPROPRIATE TECHNOLOGY IN REVIEW

STUDY SKILLS

This unit introduces students to the idea that test taking involves more than reviewing on the night before the test. Students will learn some strategies for test preparation and try out some test taking skills such as surveying the test and organizing questions by level of difficulty. Unit VIII also suggests to students that understanding how to work through different kinds of test questions (multiple choice, true/false) will help them become more skilled and effective test takers.

APPROPRIATE TECHNOLOGY

Unit VIII asks students to demonstrate their understanding of the concepts presented in Units I through VII of this book. This summary exercise will prepare students for later units in which they will apply many of these ideas to their own projects in appropriate technology.

NOTES ABOUT TEACHING UNIT VIII

1. The test on Units I–VII is found in the Teacher's Guide only. You may choose to use it in one of two ways:

   a) The test can be used as a teaching tool in the unit as well as a way of finding out what students have learned about appropriate technology. To use it in this way, you would give students portions of the test to use in Exercises II, III, and IV. You may want to have students work in pairs or alone on some or all of these exercises.

   b) The test can be used as a test only and given as a whole at the end of this unit. In this case, you would need to substitute another test in Exercise II for students to survey and some multiple choice and true/false questions in Exercise III on which students can practice their test taking skills. The test provided on Units I–VII would then be given to students in Exercise IV.

2. This unit will require two class periods to teach. Note that Exercise I is a homework assignment. You may want to have students carry out this assignment (preparing for the test) over several days. During this time, you could begin to work on Unit IX in class.

3. This unit does not specifically address the skill of answering essay questions, although there is an essay question on the Review Test. If students are not skilled in answering essay questions, you may want to discuss how to organize and write a response to essay test questions.

   The essay question on the test can be assigned as homework or done on a separate day if students need more time.

UNIT VIII: BECOMING A SKILLED TEST TAKER and
and
APPROPRIATE TECHNOLOGY IN REVIEW

INTRODUCTION

In almost any subject you study in school, sooner or later you will probably be tested on how well you know the material. Some students don't mind tests or see them as a challenge. Others think they are a bother. Some students are frightened by tests. They feel that no matter how well they know the material, they will not do well on the test.

Good test taking skills can help you do better on tests *and* make you feel more confident about taking them. In this unit you will learn several skills which will help you show what you have learned in science. Some of the skills are general test taking skills. Others will help you with certain kinds of questions, such as multiple choice and true/false questions.

59

Suggested Directions for Unit VIII

1. Have students read the "Introduction" (page 59).

   Approximate time: 3–5 minutes

2. Read "Preparing For A Test" (page 60) aloud, or have a student read it aloud. Discuss the tips with students. Ask students if they have any other ways of preparing for a test that have been successful for them.

5–10 minutes

3. Ask students to do Exercise I (page 60) for homework. If you plan to give the Unit I–VII Review Test as a separate test, announce the test date. In either case, give students enough time to prepare for the test.

When students have completed Exercise I, discuss their experiences in preparing for this test. Was it time consuming? Helpful? How might they improve?

10 minutes (for discussion)

TAKING COMMAND OF THE TEST

Once you have reviewed for a test and know the material, you can use other skills to become a better test taker.

When faced with a test, most students tackle the questions in the order in which they are given. Sometimes they are slowed down by difficult questions and never reach questions they could have answered towards the end of the test.

You can avoid this problem by TAKING COMMAND OF THE TEST. To do this, start by quickly reading over the test from beginning to end. Like surveying before you read, this gives you an idea of what to expect.

As you survey the test, fit each question into one of these four categories. This will help you organize how you will answer the questions.

1. *Quick and easy questions* — Questions you know the answer to right away that take little time to answer.

   These will probably be multiple choice, true/false, or short answer questions. Answer these questions as you find them.

2. *Easy but time consuming questions* — Questions to which you know the answer but which will take more time.

   These questions may involve solving a math problem or writing a short essay. Don't stop surveying the test to answer these questions. Instead, put a check (✓) in the margin next to these questions and go on with the survey. Once you have surveyed the test and answered all of the quick and easy questions, go back and answer the questions you have checked.

3. *Hard questions* — Questions you are not sure you know the answer to or problems you're not sure you can solve.

   When you find these questions as you survey the test, put an "x" in the margin next to them. Work on these questions only after you have answered those in groups 1 and 2.

4. *Impossible questions* —

   You may have forgotten to study for these questions, or you may not understand them. Maybe you just can't remember the answer. No matter what the reason, when you find these questions during your survey, put a question mark (?) next to them. Work on these questions only when you have answered all of the other questions.

WARNING: Don't spend too much time dividing up the test questions into these four groups. If you can't make up your mind about a question, put it in the harder of the two groups you are considering and go on. Remember: You only earn points by answering questions, not by grouping them!

If you are not allowed to write on the test, use scrap paper for your survey.

61

---

4. Read "Taking Command Of The Test" (page 61) aloud, or have students take turns reading it aloud. Clarify how to survey and categorize test questions.

   5 minutes

5. Ask students to read the directions to Exercise II (page 62). Give them a copy of the Unit I-VII Review Test or another test if you plan to give the entire Review Test at the end of the unit. Then, have them complete Exercise II. Remind students to answer only those questions for which they know the answers immediately and to categorize the others. Allow students only seven or eight minutes to complete this exercise. When they have finished, discuss their experiences in surveying and categorizing.

   NOTE: Explain to students that this process may take them some time at first. They may need to keep the categories in front of them, and they may need a few extra minutes for the test. As students become more skilled with this process, they will be able to do it more quickly. They will find that it will ultimately save them time in many testing situations.

   15 minutes

6. Read ''Multiple Choice And True/False Questions'' (page 62) aloud, or have students take turns reading it aloud. Discuss as necessary.

   5 minutes

77

7. Ask students to read the directions to Exercise III (page 63) and complete it, using the multiple choice and true/false questions on the Unit I–VII Review Test or other questions you provide for them. When they have finished, discuss their answers and how they used the suggestions on page 62 to help them answer the questions.

   10–15 minutes

8. Read "Other Test-Taking Tips" (page 63) aloud, or have students read it aloud. Discuss as necessary. Students may have other tips — things to do and not to do when taking tests — to share with classmates.

   Have students read the directions for Exercise IV (page 63). If you have not already done so, give students a copy of the Unit I–VII Review Test. If students have been working with the Review Test throughout the unit, have them use this time to complete the short answer and essay questions. If students are taking the entire test at this time, give them a full class period to complete it. When they have finished, review both the answers and the test taking skills students used to complete the test. This review may take place the day after students take the test.

   40 minutes

UNIT VIII SUMMARY

Preparing for tests

Part of being a good test taker is preparing in advance for the test.

1. Look over notes and assignments several times.

2. Keep notes and assignments in chronological order (by date).

3. The first time you review, underline main ideas and key words. Each time you review, you can focus on what you have underlined.

4. Review unit summaries.

Taking command of the test

When you get to the test, first survey and categorize the questions.

1. Answer *quick and easy questions* right away.

2. Check (✔) *easy but time consuming questions.* Go back to them as soon as you have surveyed the test and answered the quick and easy questions.

3. Put an "x" next to *hard questions.* Answer them after you have done the easier ones.

4. Put a question mark (?) next to *impossible questions.* Try these questions after you have answered all of the others.

Multiple choice and true/false questions

You can be a better test taker if you know how to answer different kinds of questions.

Multiple choice questions: Read the question and try to think of the answer before reading the choices. Read *all* of the choices, and pick the *best* answer. If you are not sure of the answer, cross out the choices you think are wrong and choose the best remaining answer.

True/false questions: If the statement is partly false, mark it false. Watch out for key words such as *always, often,* or *never.* These words can help you decide if the statement is true or false.

Other tips for test takers

1. Keep aware of your time.

2. Beware of "quicksand questions." Don't get stuck on one question; go on to the next. You can always come back if there is time.

3. Put your memory on automatic for answers that seem to be on the tip of your tongue.

4. Read directions and questions carefully.

5. Draw diagrams to help organize ideas and answers.

64

9. Review the Unit VIII Summary (page 64) with students.

REVIEW TEST   UNITS I–VII
APPROPRIATE TECHNOLOGY

Part I (Each correct answer is worth 2 points)

Directions: Circle "F" if you think a statement is a **fact**. Circle "O" if you think it is an **opinion**.

F O 1. The United States would be much better off if it did not use three billion barrels of its own petroleum each year.

F O 2. The sun's energy can be used to produce electricity.

F O 3. Most of the energy we use should come from non-renewable sources of energy such as coal, petroleum and natural gas.

Directions: Circle "T" if you think a statement is **true**. Circle "F" if you think it is **false**.

T F 4. The residential sector of the U.S. economy uses the most energy.

T F 5. Biomass is a renewable energy source.

Part II (Each correct answer is worth 2 points)

Directions: Circle the letter of the statement which best completes the sentence.

6. A technology is appropriate if it
   a) harms the environment in which it is used.
   b) lets you get things done faster.
   c) puts people out of work.
   d) uses local talents and resources.

7. A technology is inappropriate if it
   a) seriously damages the environment.
   b) uses renewable energy.
   c) uses energy efficiently.
   d) is understood, created, and maintained by the people who depend on it.

8. Appropriate technologies are usually
   a) smaller and more expensive than other technologies.
   b) larger and more expensive than other technologies.
   c) smaller and less expensive than other technologies.
   d) larger and less expensive than other technologies.

9. Communities can use appropriate technologies to
   a) pay for food grown in other states.
   b) raise taxes.
   c) solve their own problems and meet their own needs.
   d) all of the above.

10. Relying on non-renewable sources of energy makes a technology
    a) subject to shortages and cutoffs.
    b) more expensive to operate due to transportation costs.
    c) useless once the energy source is all used up.
    d) all of the above.

11. If the U.S. continues to use about three billion barrels of its own oil each year without discovering large new deposits, its proven reserves will be used up by
    a) 1992.
    b) 2005.
    c) 2105.
    d) 2585.

12. Which technology uses energy most efficiently?

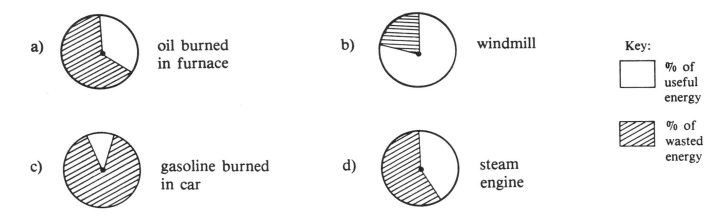

a) oil burned in furnace

b) windmill

c) gasoline burned in car

d) steam engine

Key:

☐ % of useful energy

▨ % of wasted energy

13. Which technology uses energy most efficiently?

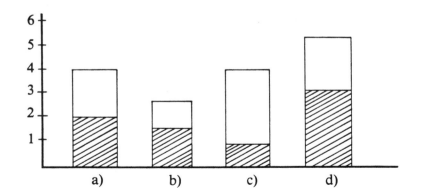

14. In what year did the imaginary country of Conservia use energy most efficiently?

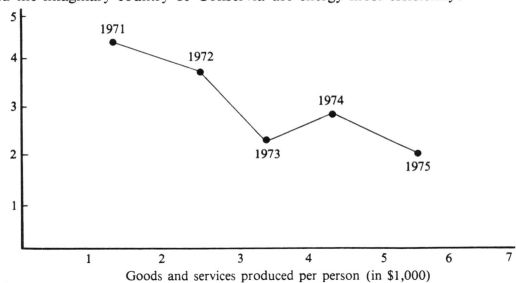

a) 1971
b) 1973
c) 1974
d) 1975

Part III (Each correct answer is worth 4 points)

Directions: Write a definition for each of the following words or phrases.

15. entropy _____

_____

_____

16. hydropower _____

_____

_____

17. proven reserves _____

_____

_____

Part IV (Each correct answer is worth 8 points)

Directions: Answer each of the following questions. Answers should be written in complete sentences except in question #22.

18. How is the planet Earth's energy supply like a spaceship's energy supply?

19. What four criteria would you use to judge how a technology affects the environment?

20. Describe three differences between renewable and non-renewable energy.

21. The city of Everett, Washington, would like to set up a system that converts trash to energy. The cost of such a system is about three million dollars. Two of the three million dollars pays for equipment which sorts the trash, separating metal, glass, paper, etc.

Everett has only one million dollars to spend on their system to convert trash to energy. Explain how this community could set up an effective system using appropriate technology that would cost only one million dollars.

22. Your family is planning to buy a new refrigerator. Before you choose one, you want to consider the life cycle costs of the refrigerators available.

In the space below, list four pieces of information (facts) you would need to know in order to make a good decision about which refrigerator to buy.

Information needed

1.

_____

2.

_____

3.

_____

4.

_____

Part V (This question is worth up to 20 points)

Directions: Write an essay of 100 to 200 words describing an appropriate technology which could be used in your community. Tell what the technology is, and explain what it is used for. Then, give all the reasons why it is an appropriate technology for your community. Use the paper provided.

(Feel free to draw a diagram if it will help you!)

Answers to Review Test, Units I–VII

Part I

1. O
2. F
3. O
4. F
5. T

Part II

6. d
7. a
8. c
9. c
10. d
11. a
12. b
13. c
14. d

Part III

15. Entropy is the amount of energy which has been lost through conversion and is unavailable for work.

16. Hydropower is a technology for using the energy contained in falling water to produce electricity or perform mechanical work.

17. Proven reserves are that portion of an oil, coal, or natural gas deposit which can be sold for more than it presently costs to extract and prepare it for sale.

Part IV (Students' answers will vary. Below are the general ideas which should be included in their responses.)

18. The earth's energy supply is like a space ship's energy supply in that both are limited. In both, we need to conserve the energy we have so we do not run out. This is especially true if the earth continues to rely on non-renewable energy sources.

19. The four criteria used to judge how a technology affects the environment are:

    1) The technology should have little immediate or long term effect on living things.

    2) The technology should not make the environment smell or look unpleasant.

    3) The environment should be able to recover quickly from the technology.

    4) The technology should not produce a lot of waste material.

20. Three differences between renewable and non-renewable energy are:

    1) Non-renewable energy is finite; renewable energy is replaced almost as fast as it is used.

    2) Renewable energy has less harmful effect on the environment than non-renewable energy.

    3) Non-renewable energy sources are subject to cutoffs and shortages; renewable sources are not.

21. Student answers will vary but should include the idea that if people in the community could sort their own trash, either at home or at a centrally located place, they could avoid spending two million dollars on sorting equipment.

22. Information needed:

    1) first cost of refrigerators

    2) operating costs of refrigerators (electricity costs)

    3) durability of each refrigerator; how long each will last

    4) reliability of each refrigerator; costs for maintenance and repair

    5) replacement costs

Part V

23. Students' answers will vary. In the essay, students should describe the technology and what it does and provide several reasons why it is appropriate (considering life cycle cost, effect on environment, use of locally available and simple technology, use of renewable energy sources, efficiency).

PART TWO:

THE SOLAR GREENHOUSE AS AN APPROPRIATE TECHNOLOGY

UNIT IX: USING SCIENTIFIC MEASURING TOOLS
and
TRAPPING THE SUN'S ENERGY

STUDY SKILLS

This unit introduces students to two measuring tools, the thermometer and the protractor, which are useful in the science classroom. It then gives students the opportunity to use these tools in a set of experiments about the solar greenhouse.

THE SOLAR GREENHOUSE: TRAPPING THE SUN'S ENERGY

In this unit, students carry out a sequence of experiments which illustrate how a solar greenhouse traps and retains the sun's energy. Through these experiments, students discover the following principles for solar greenhouse design and construction:

1. A solar greenhouse has the potential to collect more energy than it needs for its own use. The excess energy can be used to help heat an adjoining building. This excess energy will be available, however, only if the greenhouse takes full advantage of the shorter intervals of daylight experienced during the winter months. The south slope of a solar greenhouse should therefore face within 30 degrees east or west of true south, the point on the horizon above which the sun reaches the highest point in its arc across the sky.

2. The sun's ability to heat the air inside a solar greenhouse is greatest when its rays strike the south sloping glass at a perpendicular angle. In order for this to occur between the hours of 9:00 a.m. and 3:00 p.m. throughout the winter months, the glass should be tilted up from the horizontal at an angle ranging from 50 degrees in the southern U.S. to 70 degrees along the Canadian border.

3. For a solar greenhouse to share surplus energy with the adjoining building, it must be efficient in its own use of energy. All exterior surfaces should be well insulated and tightly constructed to minimize heat loss to the outside air. This pertains to the window area as well, which should have two layers of glass throughout most of the U.S. and three layers in the extreme northern states. An air space is needed between the layers of glass. Some sort of night insulation such as a shutter or roll-down shade will make the windows even more energy efficient.

The solar greenhouse is an excellent example of appropriate technology because it uses a locally available and renewable source of energy. It has minimal impact on the environment, is efficient, and is easy to understand and construct. The solar greenhouse is a technology which fosters self-sufficiency in both heat and food production.

NOTE: This unit will take two or three class periods to teach.

UNIT IX: USING SCIENTIFIC MEASURING TOOLS
and
TRAPPING THE SUN'S ENERGY

INTRODUCTION

The solar greenhouse is one example of an appropriate technology.

- It is fairly simple to build and use.
- It uses sunlight, which is a locally available and renewable energy source.
- It has little, if any, harmful effect on the environment.

In the next four units, you will experiment with some of the ideas which go into making and using a solar greenhouse.

Unit IX will show you how to use two scientific measuring tools — a thermometer and a protractor — which will help you experiment with solar energy.

READING THERMOMETERS

You have probably used a thermometer at home to find out the temperature outside or to see if you had a fever. A thermometer is also a useful scientific tool.

In a thermometer, the liquid inside the glass tube expands when it is heated and contracts or shrinks when it cools. The scale printed on the thermometer helps you "read" the temperature. The position of the liquid on the scale is the temperature of the air, water, or whatever it is you are measuring.

Example: The thermometer below shows a reading of 30°C.

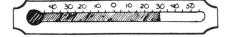

65

Suggested Directions for Unit VIII

1. Organize your class into groups of two, three, or four. Group size in this unit may depend on the amount of equipment you have available for the experiments in Exercises III and IV.

2. Ask students to read the "Introduction" (page 65) and "Reading Thermometers" (page 65). Answer any questions students have about these readings.

Approximate time: 5 minutes

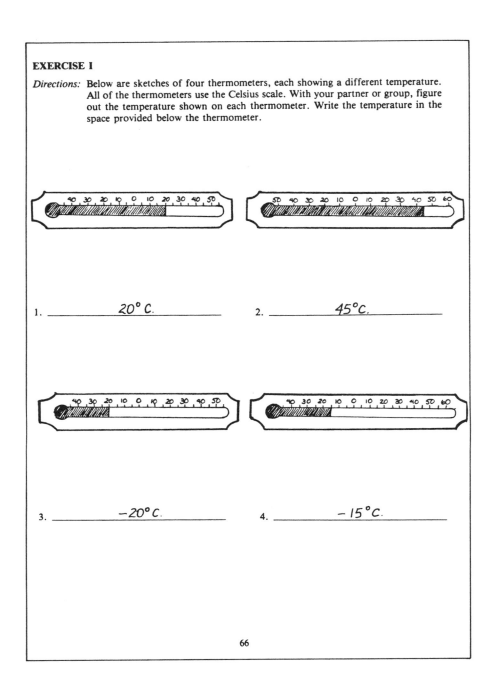

EXERCISE I

Directions: Below are sketches of four thermometers, each showing a different temperature. All of the thermometers use the Celsius scale. With your partner or group, figure out the temperature shown on each thermometer. Write the temperature in the space provided below the thermometer.

1. _____ 20° C. _____

2. _____ 45°C. _____

3. _____ −20° C. _____

4. _____ −15° C. _____

66

3. Have students read the directions for Exercise I (page 66) and complete the exercise in their groups. When students have finished, ask several of them to share their answers with the class. Discuss as necessary.

10 minutes

PROTRACTORS: MEASURING ANGLES

Sometimes you need to be able to measure the size of an angle in order to do a scientific experiment. Angles are measured in degrees, as in the samples shown below.

You use a protractor to measure angles. Look at the drawing of the protractor below as you read the explanation of how to use it.

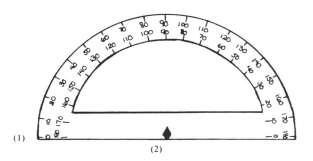

(1)

(2)

Explanation:

- All protractors have a flat edge (1) with a mark exactly in the center (2).

- The curved edge of the protractor is marked off in degrees. 0° is on the flat edge of the protractor, and 90° is at the top of the curve.

- A protractor may have two scales. The scale that starts with the 0 at the right is used to measure angles that open to the right:

  The scale with the 0 at the left is used to measure angles that open to the left:

- To measure an angle, place the flat edge of the protractor along one line of the angle. The center mark should be on the point where the two lines meet. Follow the other line of the angle out to where it crosses the scale you are using. The point on the scale where the line crosses is the measure of the angle.

67

4. Read "Protractors: Measuring Angles" (page 67) aloud, or have a student read it aloud. Give each student a protractor, and go over the Example on page 68.

5 minutes

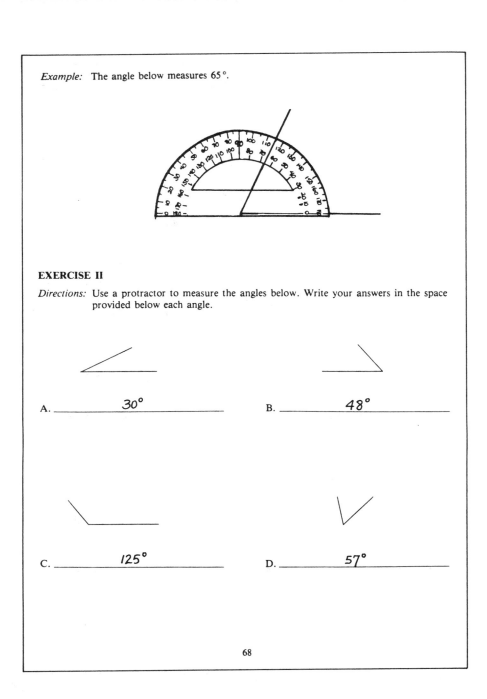

Example: The angle below measures 65°.

EXERCISE II

Directions: Use a protractor to measure the angles below. Write your answers in the space provided below each angle.

A. _____ 30° _____   B. _____ 48° _____

C. _____ 125° _____   D. _____ 57° _____

68

5. Ask students to read the directions for Exercise II (page 68) and complete it with their group. Discuss student answers as necessary.

10–15 minutes

92

EXERCISE III

Directions: In this exercise you and your partner or group will do an experiment that will show you how solar energy can be "trapped" and used to heat air. In this experiment you will A) SET UP, B) GATHER AND RECORD DATA, and C) DRAW CONCLUSIONS. Follow the steps below to carry out this experiment.

A. SETTING UP

1. Gather the following materials:

   2 thermometers
   a protractor
   a notebook
   a dark cardboard divider and a piece of cardboard large enough to shade the notebook
   a large glass jar with a screw-on lid
   a watch or clock
   pencil
   a light source (you will use sunlight or a lamp provided by your teacher)

2. If your teacher has not yet done so, use a hammer and nail to make a hole in the lid of the jar into which one thermometer fits. To do this, remove the lid from the jar and carefully hammer the nail through it. Make the hole large enough for the thermometer by moving the nail around.

3. If you are using the sun as your light source, take your materials outside and find a level place to set up. If you are using a lamp, clear a space on which to work.

4. Insert the cardboard divider into the jar. Put the lid on, and insert the thermometer through the hole in the jar lid. Tilt the jar and prop it up so that it receives direct light all along one side. Make sure the cardboard is between the light source and the thermometer. The divider will keep the light from hitting the thermometer directly. Use a protractor to measure the angle the bottom of the jar makes with the level surface. Write the angle you have measured here: _____

5. Place a notebook on the ground next to the jar. Immediately prop the second piece of cardboard so it completely shades the notebook. Then, place the second thermometer on the shaded notebook.

(Continued on page 70)

69

6. Exercise III (page 69-71) asks students to prepare, carry out, and analyze an experiment. Before students begin:

   a. Have the following equipment ready for each group or pair:

      2 thermometers
      glass jar with screw-on lid
      protractor
      light source (preferably the sun, but a 200 watt bulb will work)
      cardboard

   Each jar lid must have a hole in it through which the thermometer can be inserted. Punch a hole in the lid by removing it from the jar, placing it on a stack of folded newspapers, and hammering a nail through. Enlarge the hole by moving the nail around. You may choose to punch the holes yourself, ask one or two students to do it for the whole class, or have each group do its own.

   Each jar must also have a cardboard divider to keep the sun or light source from striking the thermometer directly. The cardboard divider should have holes in it or be cut so that air can flow from one side to the other. You may prepare these for each group or pair, or have the students make them. Their jars should look like this:

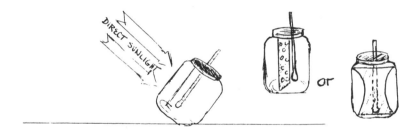

(continued)

93

b. Explain to students that the overall purpose of the experiment is to see how a solar greenhouse traps solar energy.

c. Briefly describe the steps in the experiment. These steps are described in detail in the student text, but many students find it helpful to have heard all the procedures before they read and carry them out one at a time.

B. GATHERING AND RECORDING DATA

1. Write down the following pieces of information in the spaces provided:

   Temperature outside when you start the experiment: _____

   Temperature in the jar when you start the experiment: _____

2. You are going to check the temperature of the air inside the jar and the temperature of the air outside the jar every 2 minutes for 10 minutes. Use the data table below to write down the temperatures you read every 2 minutes.

TIME	TEMPERATURE IN THE JAR	TEMPERATURE OUTSIDE THE JAR
0 minutes		
2 minutes		
4 minutes		
6 minutes		
8 minutes		
10 minutes		

3. After you have recorded the temperatures for 10 minutes, have your partner stand in the spot where his or her shadow blocks the sun from the jar (or turn off the light). Continue to read the temperatures inside and outside the jar every 2 minutes for the next 10 minutes as you did before, recording your information on the data table continued below.

TIME	TEMPERATURE IN THE JAR	TEMPERATURE OUTSIDE THE JAR
10 minutes		
12 minutes		
14 minutes		
16 minutes		
18 minutes		
20 minutes		

70

Have students complete the experiment in Exercise III, recording the data they gather in the data tables on page 70. An optional exercise at this point that may help students organize and analyze their data is to have them graph the results of their experiment. By graphing the temperatures inside and outside the jar over time on the same graph, students will be able to *see* the differences. Their graphs would look something like this:

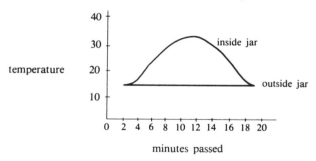

NOTE: This graph is not included in the student text.

C. DRAWING CONCLUSIONS

Use the information on your data tables to answer the questions below.

1. Which was hotter after 10 minutes, inside the jar or outside the jar?

   Students should find that it was hotter inside the jar.

2. Why do you think this happened?

   Student answers will vary. See Greenhouse Effect below.

3. What happened to the temperatures when the shadow was on the jar?

   Inside the jar: _temperature remains constant_

   Outside the jar: _temperature decreases (more rapidly than inside the jar)_

4. Why do you think this happened?

   Student answers will vary. See Greenhouse Effect below.

THE GREENHOUSE EFFECT

What you have observed in this experiment is the GREENHOUSE EFFECT. When light passes through glass and touches cool surfaces, most of it changes to heat. As heat, it cannot leave the jar as easily as it entered, so the temperature in the jar rises. A solar greenhouse works in the same way that your jar did to trap the sun's energy and change it into heat. The cartoon on page 72 may help you understand the greenhouse effect.

In the experiment in Exercise III, you had to tilt the jar to let in as much sun as possible. Then you measured the angle between the jar and the ground. When you compare this angle to those of your classmates, you will probably find that they are about the same. The best angle for catching the sun depends on how high the sun is above the horizon. If you did this experiment again at another time of day, you would probably choose a different angle to tilt the jar. If you did the experiment during another season of the year, or in a different place on earth, the best angle would again be different.

If you were building a solar greenhouse, you would have to find the best angle for catching the sun. The greenhouse should be positioned so that most of the glass faces south. The glass should be tilted so that it traps as much solar energy as possible during the winter months. You would also have to watch out for trees and buildings which might cast a shadow on the greenhouse during the winter, cutting it off from its energy source.

71

When students have gathered and recorded their data, have them answer the questions in "Drawing Conclusions" (page 71). These questions could be assigned for homework and discussed the next day. Discuss students' findings and their explanations for what they saw happening.

30–40 minutes

NOTE: There are no correct answers for the experiment in this exercise. Students' answers will vary, but they should be similar from group to group.

7. Read "The Greenhouse Effect" (page 71) aloud, or have a student read it aloud. Discuss how the cartoon on page 72 illustrates the greenhouse effect. Have students report the angle measurements they took in the experiment in Exercise III. Discuss how the angle would be different at different times of the day, in different seasons, and at different places.

10 minutes

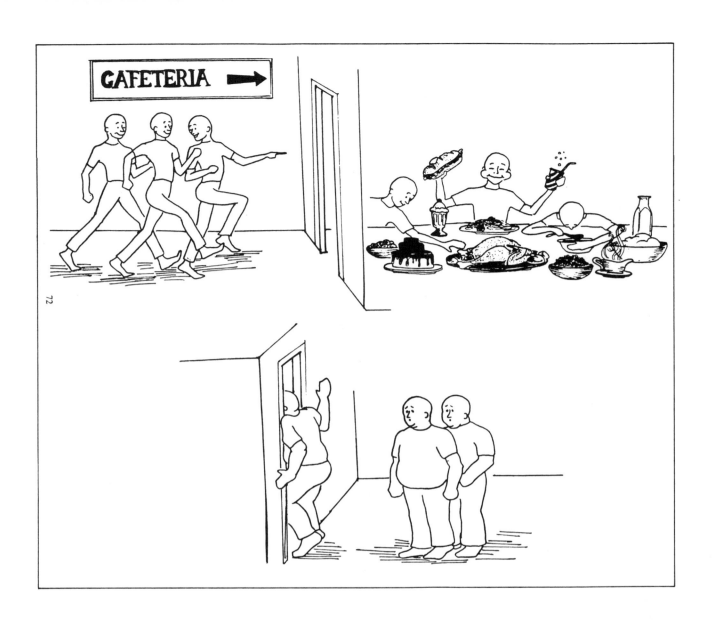

INSULATION

Glass is good at trapping heat but not good at holding it. A solar greenhouse uses INSULATION in the walls and roof to keep the heat in during the winter and out in the summer. Some solar greenhouses also use insulation over the glass on winter nights.

EXERCISE IV

Directions: Follow the steps below to carry out an experiment about insulating a solar greenhouse.

1. You will need these materials:
    2 jars with lids (and cardboard dividers)
    2 thermometers
    light source (sun or lamp)
    some kind of insulation (construction paper, cloth, wool)

2. Put a thermometer into each jar, and place both jars in front of the light source for 10 minutes. Be sure the cardboard dividers are inserted into the jars between the thermometers and the light source.

3. After 10 minutes, immediately wrap one of the jars with whatever insulation you have chosen and remove both jars from the light source (put them in a shady place).

4. Check the temperatures of both jars every 2 minutes for 10 minutes. Record your temperature readings in the data table below.

TIME	TEMPERATURE IN INSULATED JAR	TEMPERATURE IN UNINSULATED JAR
0 minutes (measured as soon as you put the jars in the shade)		
2 minutes		
4 minutes		
6 minutes		
8 minutes		
10 minutes		

5. Write two or three sentences that explain what happened in this experiment.

    Students will find that some materials hold heat in, so that in some cases, the insulated jar will stay warmer than the uninsulated jar.

73

---

8. Read "Insulation" (page 73) aloud, or have a student read it aloud. Discuss as necessary.

   Have students read the directions for Exercise IV (page 73). Provide students with a variety of materials they can use for insulating their jars, such as construction paper, foam, cloth, and quilting. Ask students to complete the experiment described in Exercise IV, recording data on the table on page 73. When students have completed the exercise, ask them to share their results with the class. Discuss how their findings could be applied to a solar greenhouse.

   30 minutes

UNIT IX SUMMARY

MEASURING TOOLS

Measuring tools can help you carry out scientific experiments and answer questions about things you see around you.

In a THERMOMETER, the liquid expands or contracts to show the temperature of air, water, or whatever you are measuring.

You use a PROTRACTOR to measure angles.

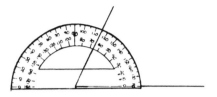

TRAPPING THE SUN: THE SOLAR GREENHOUSE

A solar greenhouse traps the sun's energy and uses it to heat the air inside. This is called the greenhouse effect. A solar greenhouse is most effective when:

1) the greenhouse faces south so that it receives as much sun as possible in the winter,

2) the glass is tilted so that as much sunlight as possible strikes it at a 90° angle for as long each day as possible, and

3) the outside surfaces of the greenhouse are well insulated and tightly built to cut down on heat loss to the outside air.

The solar greenhouse is a good example of appropriate technology. It uses a locally available and renewable source of energy. It also does little to change or hurt the environment. A solar greenhouse uses energy efficiently. It is a technology which is easy to understand and build, and one which helps people be more self sufficient in producing heat and food.

74

9. Review the Unit IX Summary (page 74) with students.

UNIT X: APPLYING SCIENTIFIC LAWS
and
HOW DOES ENERGY BEHAVE
IN A SOLAR GREENHOUSE?

STUDY SKILLS

This unit introduces students to scientific laws which describe the behavior of matter and energy. It then suggests a procedure which students can use for recognizing what scientific law is at work in a particular situation. In this procedure, students are told to:

1) OBSERVE the situation carefully,

2) RECORD their observations,

3) COMPARE their observations to other situations in which similar phenomena occurred and for which they know the law, and

4) Decide which scientific law best explains what has been observed.

This procedure is actually a variation on the problem solving scheme introduced to students in Unit VII. This could be pointed out to students and similarities and differences between the two processes discussed. This discussion may reinforce for students the idea that different problems may require different approaches and that each student may be most comfortable with a particular approach.

At the beginning of this unit, students are asked to use skills of reading and note taking introduced earlier in the book. Students have an opportunity in this unit to practice what they have learned and to apply recently learned skills to a new situation.

SCIENTIFIC LAWS AND THE SOLAR GREENHOUSE

In this unit, students are first introduced to the concept of *matter,* which is made up of *molecules.* Students learn that in solids, the molecules are very close together; in liquids they are further apart; and in gases they are quite far apart.

Students then read about and experiment with three scientific laws that determine the behavior of matter when it is heated and cooled. An understanding of these laws helps students recognize what is happening in many natural situations.

These three laws are at work in the solar greenhouse:

The Law of Conduction: When one part of a solid is warmer than another part, heat travels (conducts) from the warm area to the cooler area.

The Law of Convection:	When a liquid or gas is heated, it expands and rises. When a liquid or gas is cooled, it contracts and sinks.
The Law of Radiation:	All matter constantly emits energy in straight lines. The warmer a particle of matter is, the more energy it radiates. Particles of matter struck by radiant energy absorb heat energy and become warmer.

In a solar greenhouse, heat conducts through walls common to the greenhouse and the attached building, providing a source of heat for the building. Heat also conducts through the glass and the exterior walls of the greenhouse. Insulation must be used to slow down the rate of heat loss which results from conduction.

Convection patterns in a solar greenhouse can also be helpful or harmful. Convection can help move warm air from the greenhouse to the adjoining building. At night, however, convection can draw warm air from the house into the cooler greenhouse unless proper safeguards are taken.

Radiation also works for and against the solar greenhouse. Radiation from the sun is the energy source for the greenhouse. Radiation is also partly responsible for the transfer of heat from the greenhouse into the adjoining house through the common wall. Insulation must be used to reduce the amount of energy radiated back into space by the exterior surfaces of the greenhouse.

A NOTE ABOUT TEACHING THIS UNIT

Because this unit, like Unit IX, involves some experimentation, it will probably take two class periods to complete. We recommend that Exercise I (pages 75–80) be assigned as homework which is due on the day you wish to work on the unit in class. This allows students to make the best use of in-class time.

UNIT X: APPLYING SCIENTIFIC LAWS
and
HOW DOES ENERGY BEHAVE
IN A SOLAR GREENHOUSE?

INTRODUCTION: SCIENTIFIC LAWS

Even though you may have a few more years to go before you can get a driver's license, you probably know about the laws that tell drivers what they can and cannot do in a car.

Laws exist in science, too. Scientific laws are people's attempts to explain what happens in nature. Scientific laws cannot be broken. Energy and matter could not disobey them if they tried!

As a science student you can use scientific laws as keys for understanding nature. The more scientific laws you know and understand, the more keys you will have. The trick is knowing which key to use. This unit will help you learn the skill of applying scientific laws to what you see.

EXERCISE I

Directions: Using the skills you have learned in earlier chapters, SURVEY and READ the information on the following pages. Use the space following each section of the reading to MAP or OUTLINE that section. Then, you will be able to use the information later in the unit.

As a review of what you have read, do the REVIEW on page 80.

WHAT IS MATTER?

Matter is the "stuff" that everything is made of. It usually occurs as small clumps or bunches called *molecules.* Molecules are too small to see even with a powerful microscope.

Matter exists in three forms: *solid, liquid,* and *gas.*

When a few billion molecules are very close together, they form a *solid,* such as a rock, a tree, or a bird. Solids tend to have a definite shape.

The molecules in a *liquid,* like water, are much farther apart than they are in a solid. In a liquid, the molecules tend to take on the shape of the container which holds them.

The molecules which make up a *gas,* like air, are very far apart. The molecules of a gas tend to spread out to fill a container, like the air molecules in a balloon.

(Continued on page 76)

75

Suggested Directions for Unit X

1. Read "Introduction: Scientific Laws" (page 75) aloud, or have a student read it aloud. Discuss as necessary.

   Approximate time: 5 minutes

2. Have students read the directions to Exercise I (page 75). Assign Exercise I as homework due on the day you wish to continue work on the unit. Explain to students that they will survey, read, and map or outline the readings on pages 75 through 79 and do the Review on page 80.

(continued)

MAP OR OUTLINE:

OUTLINE:

I. Matter - what things are made of
   A. Exists as molecules
      1. Molecules close together = solid
      2. Molecules farther apart = liquid
      3. Molecules very far apart = gas

MAP:

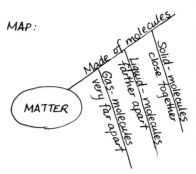

LAW OF CONDUCTION

The Law of Conduction describes how heat behaves in a solid. This law says that whenever one part of a solid is warmer than another part, heat will travel from the warm part to the cool part, until all parts of the solid are the same temperature. Conduction also explains how heat travels from one material to another when the materials are touching. These materials can be the same or different forms of matter. Heat flows from the warmer material to the cooler.

Conduction occurs whenever one molecule in a solid is warmer than the molecules next to it. The warmer molecule contains more energy, which makes it vibrate faster than the others. Because the molecules in a solid are packed closely together, the warmer, vibrating molecule bumps into its cooler neighbors. This causes them to vibrate faster and become warmer. The first molecule gives up, or conducts, some of its energy when it bumps into its neighbors. This makes it vibrate more slowly and become cooler.

Meanwhile, the other molecules have begun to vibrate faster. Each of these molecules bumps into its neighbors, transferring energy in the form of heat even further away. Conduction stops when all the molecules in a solid are vibrating at the same rate and are therefore the same temperature.

The picture below shows how conduction works.

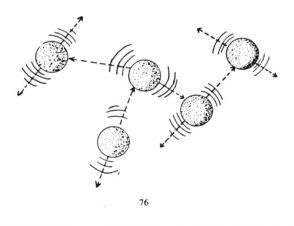

76

When students have completed Exercise I, have several of them present their maps or outlines and their examples from the Review. Discuss the laws of conduction, convection, and radiation, giving other examples to clarify these concepts if necessary. One way to demonstrate the law of conduction is to line up four or five students shoulder to shoulder at the front of the room, facing the class. Bump the student on your end hard enough to tip the student on the other end of the line off balance. Each student represents a molecule, passing its energy along to the next. If you have the students spread out so there is a foot or more between each of them and repeat the demonstration, students will see that only the first and second students are affected. This is an example of a material in which the molecules are further apart. Such a material would be a poor conductor but a good insulator.

10 minutes (for discussion)

Some solids conduct heat better than others because their molecules are closer together. Examples of good conductors are metals, concrete, and brick. Other solids are not good conductors because the molecules are farther apart. Examples of poor conductors are fiberglass, foam, and down. Poor conductors are good insulators, because they slow down the movement of heat.

MAP OR OUTLINE:

OUTLINE :

I. Conduction- how heat behaves in solids
  A. Heat travels from warm to cool part of solid
    1. Warm molecules bump cool ones and pass energy
    2. Stops when all molecules are same temperature
  B. Some solids conduct heat better than others
    1. Bad conductors are good insulators

MAP:

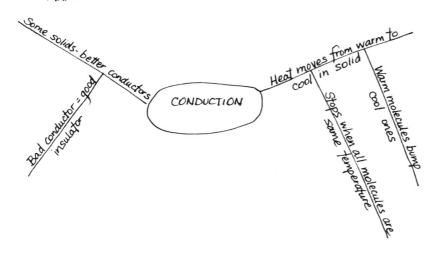

(Continued on page 78)

77

103

LAW OF CONVECTION

The Law of Convection explains what happens when a liquid or gas is heated. This law says that when a liquid or gas is heated, it expands and rises. When a liquid or gas is cooled, it shrinks, or contracts, and sinks.

Liquids and gases are both *fluids*. The molecules of which they are made vibrate faster when they are heated, just like the molecules in a solid. But because the molecules in a liquid or gas are less tightly packed than the molecules in a solid, they tranfer heat in a different way.

When the molecules in a fluid (liquid or gas) are heated and begin to vibrate faster, they move farther away from each other. This is what we mean when we say that a liquid or gas *expands* when it is heated. As the liquid or gas molecules spread apart, they rise, so the heat is transferred upward.

The same thing happens in reverse when the molecules in a liquid or gas cool. As they vibrate more and more slowly, they move closer together. We say that the liquid or gas is *contracting*. As the molecules move closer together, they begin to sink.

MAP OR OUTLINE:

OUTLINE :

I. Law of Convection - heating liquid or gas
  A. Heat makes molecules of fluid vibrate faster
    1. When molecules vibrate faster, move away from each other - expand
    2. Molecules spread apart and float upward
    3. Heat goes up
  B. When molecules cool, vibrate more slowly
    1. Molecules get closer together - contract
    2. Molecules sink as they cool

MAP :

78

Note that in the section on the Law of Convection, the concept of density is not explicitly discussed. Students can understand the law more easily when it is presented in this way. A fluid's density, or how many molecules there are in a given volume, governs its tendency to rise or fall. The molecular weight of a material is also a factor.

LAW OF RADIATION

The Law of Radiation says that matter gives off or *radiates* energy all of the time. The warmer matter is, the more energy it radiates. When other matter is hit by this radiating energy, it becomes warmer.

When a material is heated, the molecules on its surface vibrate faster. These molecules then give off energy which travels in straight lines in all directions. When this energy reaches the molecules in another object, it starts these molecules vibrating faster and raises their temperatures.

Radiation is a way of transferring energy from one piece of matter to another without the vibrating molecules touching each other or moving from one place to another. As the picture below shows, you don't have to touch the stove to get warm, because it radiates energy.

MAP OR OUTLINE:

OUTLINE:
I. Law of Radiation
   A. Matter gives off energy
   B. Warm matter radiates more energy than cool matter.
      1. Molecules on surface vibrate faster
      2. Molecules give off energy in straight lines
      3. When radiated energy hits other matter, new
         molecules vibrate faster – object gets warmer

MAP:

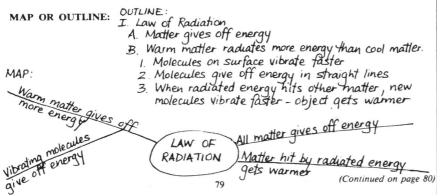

Warm matter gives off more energy

Vibrating molecules give off energy

LAW OF RADIATION

All matter gives off energy

Matter hit by radiated energy gets warmer

79

(Continued on page 80)

105

> **REVIEW:** Look back over the notes you have taken. With a partner, choose *one* of the scientific laws explained in the readings. Think of an example from your own experience in which you saw the scientific law operating. Write a few sentences below that describe your example.
>
> LAW: _Student responses will vary. Accept any reasonable responses. Some_
>
> EXAMPLE: _possible responses are:_
>
> _Law of Conduction: Using a hot water bottle to warm the bed._
>
> _Law of Convection: Top floors of house are warmer in summer as heat rises_
>
> _Law of Radiation: Heat given off by sun._
>
> _____
>
> _____
>
> ### RECOGNIZING SCIENTIFIC LAWS
>
> To recognize scientific laws as they operate, you can use the three step process of OBSERVING, RECORDING, and COMPARING described below.
>
> 1) OBSERVE what is going on in the situation. Every movement, color, sound, smell, taste, and touch can tell you something.
>
> 2) RECORD your observations. You may be able to remember many details, but the best way to remember all of them is to write them down. Sometimes there may not be enough time to record everything.
>
> 3) COMPARE your observations to other situations in which you saw similar things happening. What law was operating in those situations? Decide which scientific law best explains what you observed and recorded.
>
> ### EXAMPLES OF THE LAW OF CONDUCTION
>
> You have experienced the law of conduction many times. Perhaps you have had one of these experiences:
>
> 1. You leave a cool spoon in a bowl of hot soup. When you pick up the spoon, it has become very hot. Heat has been transferred from the soup to the spoon and up the handle according to the law of conduction.
>
> 2. You lean your arm on the desk for a long period of time. When you lift it up, you find that the place where your arm has been is warm. Heat has been conducted from your arm to the desk top.
>
> Exercises II and III will show you examples of the laws of convection and radiation.
>
> 80

The Review (page 80) can be done in several ways. Students can be assigned or choose a partner to work with, and the Review can be done with the readings in Exercise I as homework. Students are responsible for calling or meeting with their partner to complete the Review. OR, students can be given 5–10 minutes to complete the Review at the beginning of the class following the homework assignment. A third option is to have students complete the Review individually.

3. Organize the class into groups of three or four.

   Read "Recognizing Scientific Laws" (page 80) aloud, or have a student read it aloud. Discuss how this process is similar to and different from the problem solving process presented in Unit VII.

   5 minutes

4. Have students read "Examples Of The Law Of Conduction" (page 80). Discuss as necessary. Ask students for other examples.

   5 minutes

EXERCISE II

Directions: Your teacher will demonstrate another scientific law for you. Follow the steps below to see if you can recognize what it is.

1. OBSERVE what the teacher does.

2. Use this space to RECORD what you see happening:

3. COMPARE this to other situations that seemed similar.

4. Which scientific law does this experiment show? _____

_____

EXERCISE III

Directions: Follow the steps below to see a third scientific law at work.

SET UP

1. You will need: a light bulb (plugged in)
   a piece of cardboard

(Continued on page 82)

81

---

5. Have students read the directions and steps for Exercise II (page 81). Carry out the following demonstration of the law of convection.

   1) Fill a beaker with water and place it on a rack. Place a Bunsen burner under the beaker so that the flame is to one side of the center of the beaker (see picture above).

   2) Let the water come to a boil. Instruct students first to observe and then to record what they see happening next.

   3) Drop a small handful of sawdust into the boiling water. Give students a few minutes to observe the results.

   4) Ask students to complete Exercise II.

When students have finished, ask several to explain what they saw and what law of heat transfer was demonstrated.

10–15 minutes

6. Have students read the directions for Exercise III (page 81) and complete it in their groups. When they have finished, ask a member of each group to share her or his group's findings and conclusions with the class. Discuss how this experiment illustrates the law of radiation.

10–15 minutes

107

OBSERVE AND RECORD

2. Plug in the light bulb. Hold your hand to one side of the bulb without touching it.

   What happens to the temperature of your hand? _hand gets warmer;_

   _____temperature goes up_____

3. Leave your hand to one side of the light bulb. Hold the cardboard between your hand and the bulb.

   What happens to the temperature of your hand? __cools_____

   _____

COMPARE

4. Can you think of other situations in which you experienced something similar? What laws were in action in those situations? Discuss this with your group.

5. What scientific law does this experiment show? _Law of Radiation_____

   _____

82

SCIENTIFIC LAWS AND THE SOLAR GREENHOUSE

The solar greenhouse operates according to the scientific laws of conduction, convection, and radiation. Remember:

One example of *conduction* is the transfer of heat through solid matter.

Convection is the transfer of heat in a liquid or gas. Heated fluids expand and rise. Cooled fluids contract and sink.

Radiation is the transfer of energy from the surface of an object into space.

The arrows in the solar greenhouse below show where conduction is occurring. Read the explanation as you look at the picture.

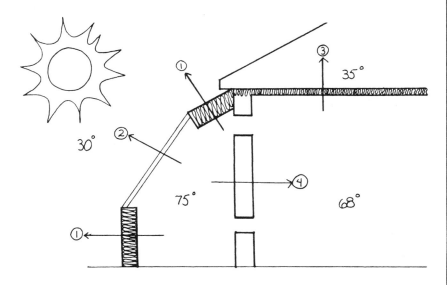

Explanation:
- Heat is conducted through walls and roof to the outside (arrows #1). If walls contain materials that are poor conductors (insulation), heat will be lost more slowly.
- Heat is conducted through the glass to the outside (arrow #2). If there are two layers of glass with an air space between them, heat will be lost more slowly.
- Heat is conducted through the ceiling to the attic (arrow #3). Again, insulation here would slow down heat loss.
- Heat is conducted through the wall to the house, helping to heat the house (arrow #4).

83

7. Read "Scientific Laws And The Solar Greenhouse" (page 83) aloud, or have a student read it aloud. Discuss with students how the arrows in the picture of a solar greenhouse on page 83 show where conduction occurs.

5-10 minutes

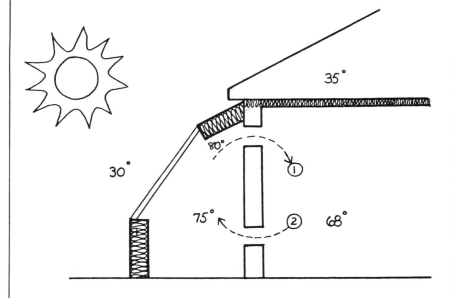

EXERCISE IV

Directions: The pictures below and on the next page show the same solar greenhouse as on page 83. Each picture has arrows which show a scientific law of heat transfer in action. For each picture:

1) Observe - look carefully to see what is happening.

2) Record what is happening at each arrow in the space provided.

3) Compare what you have recorded to the examples of scientific laws in Exercises II and III.

4) Explain which scientific law is shown by the arrows.

Picture 1

1. Observe what is happening.

2. Record: What is happening at arrow #1? *Warm air rises and goes into house.*

_____

What is happening at arrow #2? *Cool air sinks and re-enters greenhouse, replacing the air that has left the greenhouse.*

84

8. Ask students to read the directions to Exercise IV (page 84). Have students complete the exercise in their groups. When they have finished, discuss their responses to the questions on pages 84–86. Students should be able to explain what law of heat transfer each arrow represents. Discuss what would happen in each picture if a) it were night and/or b) temperatures outside, in the greenhouse, and in the building were different (see the additional suggestions at the end of this unit for pictures of these situations).

15–20 minutes

3. Which example from Exercises II and III is similar to what you see happening with these arrows? _Exercise II with water in beaker._

How are they alike? _Both show warm fluid rising and cold sinking._

4. Which scientific law do these arrows show? _Law of Convection_

Picture 2

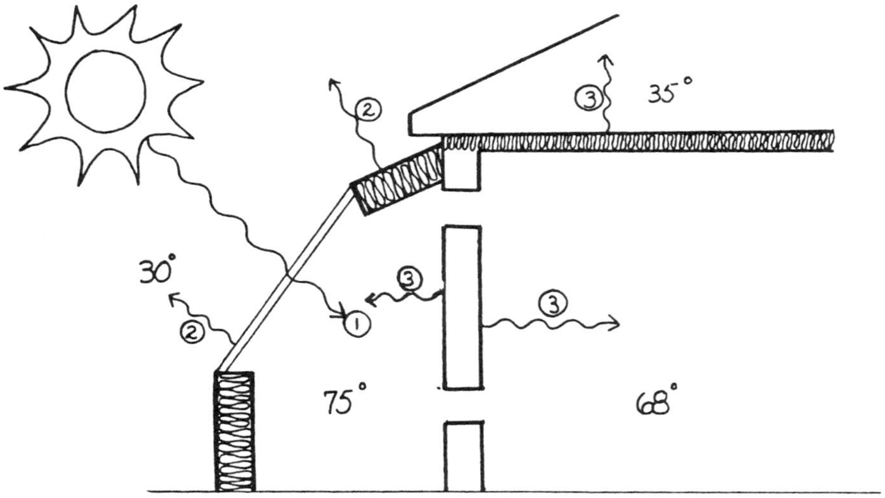

1. Observe what is happening.

2. Record: What is happening at arrow #1? _Sun radiates energy_

What is happening at the arrows marked #2? _Glass and walls radiate energy out into space._

What is happening at the arrows marked #3? _Common wall radiates energy; ceiling radiates energy into attic._

(Continued on page 86)

85

111

3. Compare: Which example from Exercises II and III is similar to what you see happening in this picture? *Exercise III with light bulb.*

_____

How are they alike? *Both show energy radiated from warm matter to cooler matter*

4. Which scientific law do the arrows in this picture show? _____
Law of Radiation

UNIT X SUMMARY

APPLYING SCIENTIFIC LAWS:

To figure out which scientific law is operating in a situation, follow these steps:

OBSERVE what is happening.

RECORD all of your observations.

COMPARE what you see to other situations in which you know what law is operating. Then, decide which scientific law explains your observations.

SCIENTIFIC LAWS AND THE SOLAR GREENHOUSE

Scientific laws describe how matter and energy behave.

Matter is the "stuff" everything is made of. It exists in very small bunches, called *molecules.*

When the molecules are close together, the matter forms a *solid.*

When the molecules are farther apart, the matter is a *liquid.*

When the molecules are very far apart, the matter is a *gas.*

Three scientific laws of heat transfer operate in a solar greenhouse.

The *Law of Conduction:* Whenever one part of a solid is warmer than another part, heat travels from the warm part to cooler parts until the solid is all the same temperature. Through conduction, heat escapes through the solid surfaces of a solar greenhouse. To slow down this heat loss, you must use materials that are poor conductors to insulate walls and ceilings.

The *Law of Convection:* When a liquid or gas is heated, it expands and rises. When it cools, it contracts and sinks. Warm air from a solar greenhouse rises by convection and moves into the attached building. Cool air from the building moves back into the greenhouse to be reheated.

The *Law of Radiation:* Matter radiates energy in straight lines. Warm matter radiates more energy than cool matter. When matter is struck by radiant energy, it becomes warmer. A solar greenhouse receives radiant energy from the sun. At the same time, the outside surfaces of the greenhouse radiate heat back into space. Heat also radiates from the back wall of the greenhouse into the adjoining building, providing a source of heat for the building.

87

9. Review the Unit X Summary (page 87) with students.

Additional Suggestions

1. Provide students with other pictures of solar greenhouses similar to those in Exercise IV (page 84–86) but with different structures and temperatures. Several examples have been given below and on the next page. Include arrows, and ask students what they represent, OR ask students to draw in the arrows which show where conduction, convection, and radiation occur.

SAMPLE PICTURES:

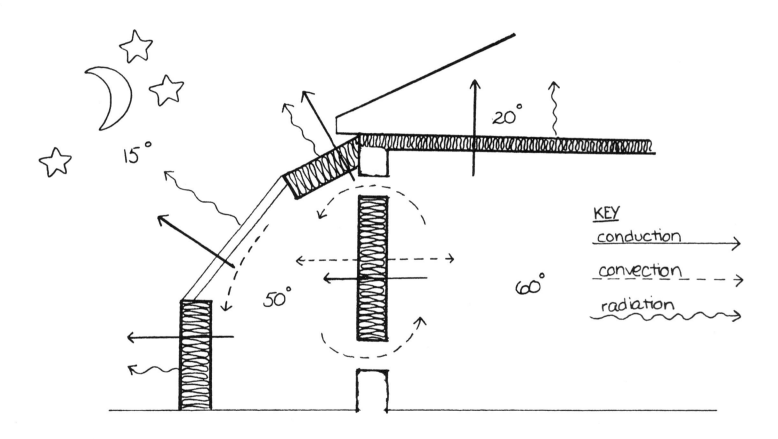

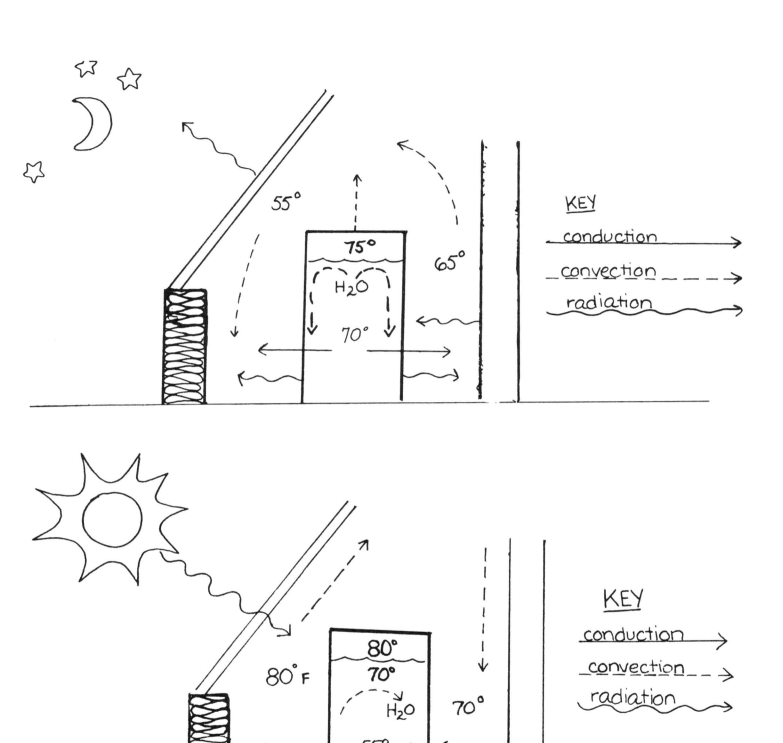

UNIT XI: WORKING WITH THE METRIC SYSTEM
and
HOW CAN WE STORE ENERGY?

STUDY SKILLS

This unit introduces students to the metric system and asks them to use metric measurements as they experiment with ways of storing solar energy. More specifically, the unit presents the meter as a unit of length, the liter as a unit of volume, and the gram as a unit of weight. It also explains that degrees Celsius is a metric measure of temperature, and that a calorie is a unit of heat (one calorie is the amount of heat needed to raise the temperature of one gram of water one degree Celsius). Prefixes such as kilo, centi, and milli are added to metric measurements to indicate the number of units.

A NOTE ABOUT TEACHING THE METRIC SYSTEM:

Any measuring system is more meaningful to students if they can visualize the units. Since the United States still relies on the English system of measurement, most American students do not "think metric." Students may find it helpful if meter sticks, liter containers, and materials measured in grams (e.g., a box of sugar or salt) are in front of them and continually referred to as they work with the metric system.

STORING SOLAR ENERGY

Non-renewable energy in the form of coal, oil, or natural gas is already stored; it is potential energy until it is burned. Renewable energy can also be stored as potential energy. Solar energy is stored in plants and trees (biomass) and in water capable of running downhill (the sun evaporates water from lakes and oceans, in effect lifting it uphill so it can run downhill). When the sun's energy takes the form of heat (thermal solar), however, storage is more problematic. Some materials are more appropriate for this purpose than others.

On a sunny winter day, a well-designed, properly sited, and carefully constructed greenhouse will collect an over-abundance of solar thermal energy. The amount of extra energy varies from state to state and even from town to town. In almost every part of the United States a solar greenhouse will overheat unless the surplus is anticipated and dealt with.

There are three ways to avoid overheating:

1. Let in some cooler outside air by opening windows and vents. This solution is inefficient and wasteful.

2. If the solar greenhouse is attached to another building, circulate the warm air through the adjoining house. This would help reduce the occupants' use of non-renewable energy.

3. Store the extra energy for use at night and on cloudy days. Materials appropriate for this purpose are called *thermal mass*.

Most attached solar greenhouses share some of their excess energy with the adjoining building and store the rest for their own use at night and on cloudy days.

In this unit, students will experiment with a variety of materials for absorbing and storing thermal solar energy. Through experimentation, students will determine which materials are most appropriate and effective when used in a solar greenhouse.

116

NOTE ABOUT TEACHING THIS UNIT:

Because this unit involves student experimentation, it will probably require two class periods.

Suggested Directions for Unit XI

1. Organize your class into groups of three or four. You may want to put one or more strong math students in each group, as several of the exercises in this unit require students to calculate their answers.

2. Read "Introduction: The Metric System" (page 88) and "Measurements In The Metric System" (page 88) aloud, or have a student read them aloud. Use examples of meters, liters, and grams to help students compare these units to English measurements. Students can look at a meter stick or a metric ruler to see how meters are divided into centimeters and millimeters.

Approximate time: 5–10 minutes

3. Have students read the directions for Exercise I (page 88) and complete the exercise in their groups. When students have finished, go over the correct answers to the four questions. Discuss any problems or questions students have about using the metric system in this exercise.

5–10 minutes

2. A meter stick is 1 meter long. How many centimeters are there on the meter stick? _____
   100 centimeters

3. A container of water weighs 4,000 grams. How many kilograms does it weigh? _____
   4 kilograms

4. A feather weighs 1 milligram. How many grams does it weigh? _1/1000 gram_

STORING SOLAR ENERGY

The solar energy entering a solar greenhouse turns into heat when it strikes the floor, the walls, and even the plants. On a sunny day, the greenhouse can quickly get too warm. There are several ways to prevent overheating. The most common one is to store the extra energy for use at night or on cloudy days.

There are many ways to store energy. A car battery stores electrical energy produced by the running engine. A watch spring stores energy when you wind it. A dam stores energy when it holds back water which can be released to generate electricity. Non-renewable energy is already stored in the form of coal, oil, and natural gas.

For a solar greenhouse to store energy, it must contain materials which can soak up heat like a sponge. Materials used in this way are called *thermal mass*. An ideal material for storing energy in a solar greenhouse would hold large amounts of heat and take up a small space. It would also be a material that loses heat slowly.

In Exercises II and III you will experiment with several different materials to see which would be most appropriate for use as thermal mass in a solar greenhouse.

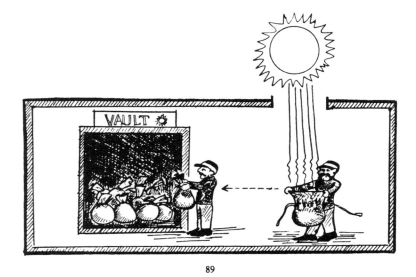

89

4. Have students read "Storing Energy" (page 89) to themselves. Discuss as necessary.
   5 minutes

EXERCISE II

Directions: Follow the steps below to carry out an experiment about how different materials store heat.

SET UP

1. You will need these materials:

   3 identical glass jars with screw-on lids (one hole in each lid)
   3 Celsius thermometers
   an energy source (sun or heat lamp)
   material to put in jars, such as sand, rock, air, water, wood chips, clay

2. Weigh the empty jars. Use a scale that measures in grams. Write the weight of each jar in the appropriate space below.

   _____   _____   _____
         Jar 1   Jar 2   Jar 3

3. Fill each jar with a different material. Weigh each jar. Record these weights in the appropriate spaces below. Then, subtract the weight of jar 1 when empty from the weight of the same jar when filled. The difference is the weight of the material in the jar. Write this number in the appropriate space. Then, do the same for jars 2 and 3.

	Material	Weight of filled jar	Weight of empty jar	Weight of material in jar
Jar 1				
Jar 2				
Jar 3				

4. Screw on the jar lids, and insert a thermometer through the hole in each lid. Place all three jars at an equal distance from the light source. Be sure that none of the jars is shaded and that all have the same amount of surface facing the light source.

OBSERVE AND RECORD

5. Record the beginning temperature of each jar in Data Table #1 on the next page. Then, measure the temperature in each jar at 2 minute intervals, recording your information in Data Table #1. Continue measuring the temperatures until all the temperatures seem to stop rising.

90

5. Have students read the directions for Exercise II (page 90). Explain that they will be doing an experiment similar to those they carried out in Unit IX. Before students begin work on Exercise II, go over the steps of the experiment with them, or have them read the entire exercise through on their own. Have necessary materials available for students. You may want to have all students experiment with the same three materials, or you may want to have different groups working with different materials.

Ask students to complete the experiment, data tables, and questions in Exercise II. When students reach the step COMPARE (page 92), you may want to help them find out what other groups have discovered about different (or similar) materials. For example, you might have a member of each group put the group's data tables on the board. Students could find the average high temperature of each material used and make a graph of all of the averages. Or, one table for each material used could be put on the board and the results compared.

When students have finished the exercise, discuss the questions on page 92. Point out that although water did not have the highest temperature, it absorbed the most heat and therefore cooled more slowly.

30–40 minutes

119

Data Table #1

	Jar 1 Material:_____	Jar 2 Material:_____	Jar 3 Material:_____
Beginning temp.			
2 minutes			
4 minutes			
6 minutes			
8 minutes			
10 minutes			
12 minutes			

6. Remove the jars from the energy source. Measure the temperatures at 2 minute intervals for 10 minutes. Record your data in Data Table #2, below.

Data Table #2

	Jar 1 Material:_____	Jar 2 Material:_____	Jar 3 Material:_____
Beginning temp.			
2 minutes			
4 minutes			
6 minutes			
8 minutes			
10 minutes			

(Continued on page 92)

EXPLAIN

7. Using the information from Data Tables #1 and #2, answer these questions:

   a) Which material reached the highest temperature? _____ **Students' answers will vary for**

   b) Which material stayed the coolest? _____ **all parts of #7.**

   c) Which material dropped the fewest number of degrees after you removed the jars from the energy source? _____

   d) Which material dropped the greatest number of degrees after you removed the jars from the energy source? _____

COMPARE

8. If other groups in your class used different materials, compare your results to theirs. Look
   for: Which material got hottest?
            Which material stayed the coolest?
            Which material had the greatest temperature drop in the given time?
            Which material had the least temperature drop?

MEASURING HEAT: CALORIES

It is possible to measure the amount of heat a material absorbs, or takes in and holds. The unit of heat in the metric system is the CALORIE.

One CALORIE is the amount of heat needed to raise the temperature of 1 gram of water 1 degree Celsius. If 1 gram of water starts at 10 degrees Celsius and is heated to 11 degrees Celsius, it has absorbed 1 calorie of heat. If it is heated to 15 degrees Celsius, it has absorbed 5 calories of heat.

To find out how many calories of heat a material has absorbed, multiply its weight in grams by the change in temperature. In the example above, 1 gram of water x 5° Celsius = 5 calories.

Example: If 100 grams of water is heated and its temperature is raised 20° Celsius, how many calories have been added?

   100 grams of water × 20° Celsius = 2,000 calories

Remember: Heat, measured in calories, and temperature, measured in degrees, are not the same. Heat depends on the amount of material. Temperature does not. A teaspoonful of water and a bathtub full of water may both be at the same temperature: 30° Celsius. But the bathtub contains more heat, or calories, and will therefore cool more slowly.

92

6. Read "Measuring Heat: Calories" (page 92) aloud, or have a student read it aloud. Go over the Example on page 92. If students need more practice, provide them with other examples that help them understand what calories are and how they can be computed.

   NOTE: The English term comparable to calorie is the BTU. It is defined as the amount of heat needed to raise the temperature of one pound of water one degree Fahrenheit.

5 minutes

EXERCISE III

Directions: Use the information you recorded in Exercise II to fill in the blanks below. First, write the name of each material you used in the spaces provided. Then, for each material, write the information asked for. This information will help you find out how much heat each material absorbed.

MATERIAL 1: *Student answers will vary depending on the type and amount of materials used.*

1. What was the weight of this material? _____ grams

2. What was the beginning temperature? _____ °Celsius

3. What was the highest temperature this material reached? _____ °Celsius

4. What was the change in temperature? (Subtract the beginning temperature from the highest temperature.) _____ °Celsius

5. Find how many calories the material absorbed. Multiply the weight in grams by the change in temperature.

    Write your result here: _____ grams × _____ °Celsius = _____ calories

MATERIAL 2: _____

1. What was the weight of the material? _____ grams

2. What was the beginning temperature? _____ °Celsius

3. What was the highest temperature this material reached? _____ °Celsius

4. What was the change in temperature (highest temperature minus beginning temperature)?
    _____ °Celsius

5. How many calories did this material absorb? (Multiply grams × change in temperature.)
    _____ grams × _____ °Celsius = _____ calories

MATERIAL 3: _____

1. What was the weight of the material? _____ grams

2. What was the beginning temperature? _____ °Celsius

3. What was the highest temperature this material reached? _____ °Celsius

4. What was the change in temperature (highest temperature minus beginning temperature)?
    _____ °Celsius

5. How many calories did this material absorb?
    _____ grams × _____ °Celsius = _____ calories

(Continued on page 94)

93

7. Have students read the directions for Exercise III (page 93). Point out that they will be using data gathered in Exercise II to find out how many calories of heat each material absorbed. Have students complete the exercise in their groups. When they have finished, discuss their answers to the questions on page 94.

15–20 minutes

Now answer these questions:

1. Which material was exposed to the most heat? _All materials were exposed to the same amount of heat_

2. Which material absorbed the most heat (the greatest number of calories)? _____
   Students' answers will vary.

3. Which material would you choose to store heat in a solar greenhouse? _____
   _____

   Why? _If water was one of the materials tested, students will usually find that it absorbed the most heat and would therefore be the most suitable material to use for heat storage in a solar greenhouse. If water was not tested, students should choose whichever material absorbed the greatest amount of heat._

   The material which absorbed the most heat would be the most appropriate choice for thermal mass in a solar greenhouse because:

   1) it would store the most heat for later use
   and
   2) it would be most effective in preventing overheating

94

123

UNIT XI SUMMARY

WORKING WITH THE METRIC SYSTEM

The metric system is a way of measuring distance, volume, weight, temperature, and heat. In the metric system:

A **meter** is a unit of length.

A **liter** is a unit of volume.

A **gram** is a unit of mass or weight.

Temperature is measured in **degrees Celsius.**

A **calorie** is a unit of heat. A calorie is the amount of heat needed to raise the temperature of 1 gram of water 1° Celsius.

In the metric system, prefixes are added to show the number of each unit being measured.

Kilo = 1,000. A kilometer = 1,000 meters.

Centi = 1/100. A centimeter = 1/100 meter. 100 centimeters = 1 meter.

Milli = 1/1,000. A millimeter = 1/1,000 meter. 1,000 millimeters = 1 meter.

STORING ENERGY IN A SOLAR GREENHOUSE

Energy can be stored for use at a later time. Non-renewable energy is already stored in the form of oil, gas, and coal.

A solar greenhouse will overheat on a sunny winter day unless something is done with the extra heat. One solution is to store the extra heat for use at night or on a cloudy day.

Materials which absorb and store heat are called *thermal mass.* Air is not an appropriate thermal mass because it cannot store very much heat without becoming too hot for a solar greenhouse. Water is a very appropriate thermal mass because it can store a lot of heat at a low temperature. It also cools very slowly.

95

8. Review the Unit XI Summary (page 95) with students.

Additional Suggestions

1. To gain more familiarity with the metric system, students might begin to examine packaged food and beverage containers. Almost all of these packages have metric as well as English units. Students could design a bulletin board displaying these labels and other uses of the metric system that they find.

2. More advanced students might want to work through the following problem to determine the amount of water storage material needed to prevent a solar greenhouse from overheating.

   Assume that this solar greenhouse is 4 meters wide, 10 meters long, and 3 meters high where the roof meets the back wall. This greenhouse can collect 60,000,000 calories of solar energy on a sunny winter day, only half of which it needs to maintain a comfortable temperature. How many liter-sized containers would be needed to store this extra heat?

   a. Water stored in a solar greenhouse usually ranges from 15°C to 25°C over the course of a sunny winter day. How many calories of heat can each gram of water absorb and store?

   $$1 \text{ gram } \times (25\text{-}15)° \text{ Celsius/gram } = 10 \text{ calories}$$

   b. How many grams of water are needed to absorb and store the extra 30,000,000 calories?

   $$30,000,000 \text{ calories } \div 10 \text{ calories/gram } = 3,000,000 \text{ grams}$$

   c. One gram of water occupies one cubic centimeter (cm³). How many cubic centimeters of water storage are needed for the amount of water you found in question b?

   $$3,000,000 \text{ grams } \times 1 \text{ gram/cm}^3 = 3,000,000 \text{ cm}^3$$

   d. One liter equals 1,000 cm³. How many liters of water storage are needed?

   $$3,000,000 \text{ cm}^3 \div 1,000 \text{ cm}^3/\text{liter } = 3,000 \text{ liters}$$

   e. The area of the back wall of the solar greenhouse is 3 meters high by 10 meters long, or 300 centimeters × 1,000 centimeters = 300,000 square centimeters. A liter measures 10 centimeters by 10 centimeters by 10 centimeters. The surface area of one side of a liter container is 10 centimeters × 10 centimeters = 100 centimeters. In question d you found out how many liters of water storage were needed in this greenhouse. Would that number of liters fit against the back wall of the greenhouse if they are stacked one on top of another one row thick?

   $$300,000 \text{ cm}^2 \div 100 \text{ cm}^2/\text{liter } = 3,000 \text{ liter containers}$$

UNIT XII: WORKING WITH LARGE NUMBERS
and
HOW CAN WE CONSERVE ENERGY?

STUDY SKILLS

To work with the large numbers involved in energy use and conservation, students need to be familiar with scientific notation. This unit introduces students to the use of scientific notation. It also gives students practice in adding, subtracting, multiplying, and dividing numbers written in scientific notation.

A NOTE ABOUT TEACHING SCIENTIFIC NOTATION

If students are not familiar with scientific notation, you will need to provide more examples and extra practice problems to supplement those given on pages 97-99 of this unit. Some extra problems have been provided in the Additional Suggestions to this unit.

This unit requires a great deal of computation. Your students will find calculators useful in multiplying and dividing the coefficients of numbers written in scientific notation. The use of calculators will not detract from the activities presented in this unit.

CONSERVING ENERGY

It serves little purpose to attach a solar greenhouse to a home or building if the extra energy produced by the greenhouse is wasted through inefficiency. This unit presents several ways in which heat can be conserved in a home or building:

- keep the furnace running efficiently,
- insulate the attic,
- install storm windows,
- close drapes at night; re-open each morning, and
- lower the thermostat when people are out or asleep.

The unit explains that heat is measured in British Thermal Units, or BTUs. One BTU is the amount of heat needed to raise one pound of water one degree Fahrenheit. Students can find out how many BTUs their home or school uses by multiplying the number of BTUs in one gallon of oil, a cubic foot of natural gas, or a kilowatt of electricity by the total number of units of fuel used.

Students are asked to work with one method of conserving energy — insulation — to see how much energy can be saved by using it and what its costs are. Examples of savings from other methods of energy conservation are included in the Teacher's Guide for this unit under Additional Suggestions. You may want to use these with your students for comparison.

After students have completed this unit, you might want them to gather information about energy loss and conservation in their homes or in the school. The formulas given can be applied in either situation and will reveal several ways in which real energy dollars can be saved through conservation.

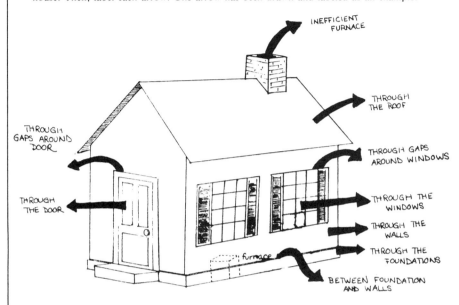

UNIT XII: WORKING WITH LARGE NUMBERS
and
HOW CAN WE CONSERVE ENERGY?

INTRODUCTION

Heat escapes from many different places in a house or building. Look at the sketch below. Draw arrows to show where you think heat escapes from this house or is wasted in this house. Then, label each arrow. One arrow has been drawn and labeled as an example.

CONSERVING ENERGY

So far you have learned about trapping and storing solar energy in a solar greenhouse. But trapping and storing energy is of little use if the energy is allowed to escape into the outside air. We also need ways of keeping energy from being lost or wasted. This is called *conserving energy*. This unit will show you several ways of conserving energy in a house or building.

96

Suggested Directions for Unit XI

1. Organize students into pairs or groups of three to four. If students are using calculators, they will need one calculator per pair or small group.

2. Have students read the "Introduction" (page 96) and draw the arrows showing heat loss. Draw a similar house on the board. When students have finished, have several come to the board and draw and label the arrows they have on their papers. Add any arrows suggested by other students or by the illustration in the picture provided above. Discuss as necessary.

   Approximate time: 10 minutes

3. Read "Conserving Energy" (page 96) aloud, or have a student read it aloud.

   2–3 minutes

WORKING WITH LARGE NUMBERS

To understand the amount of heat which enters and leaves a building, you need to be able to work with very large numbers. These numbers are too big for most hand calculators. Fortunately, scientists have developed a system of dealing with large numbers. This system is called SCIENTIFIC NOTATION.

In SCIENTIFIC NOTATION, the number 1,000,000,000,000.0 is written as 1.0×10^{12}

- Notice that in scientific notation the decimal point is moved so there is only one digit to the left of the decimal point, in this case a 1. *The number of places the decimal point has been moved is shown by the number above and to the right of the 10. This number is called the exponent. In 1×10^{12} the exponent is 12. This means the decimal has been moved 12 places to the left.*

- The number with the decimal point is called the *coefficient*.

Look at the examples below.

a) $1,000,000,000,000 = 1.0 \times 10^{12}$

where 12 is the exponent and 1.0 is the coefficient

b) $150 = 1.5 \times 10^{2}$

where 2 is the exponent and 1.5 is the coefficient

c) $1,850,000 = 1.85 \times 10^{6}$

where 6 is the exponent and 1.85 is the coefficient

EXERCISE I

Directions: In Part A, put each number into scientific notation.

In Part B, write out the number that is shown in scientific notation.

PART A	Scientific Notation
1. 1,000	1. 1×10^{3}
2. 3,250,000	2. 3.25×10^{6}
3. 43,000	3. 4.3×10^{4}

PART B	Number Written Out
4. 6×10^{5}	4. 600,000
5. 1.2×10^{2}	5. 120
6. 7.32×10^{3}	6. 7320

97

4. Read "Working With Large Numbers" (page 97) aloud, or have a student read it aloud. Go over the examples on page 97. Provide other examples if necessary.

If students are not already familiar with rounding off, you may want to show them how to round off in scientific notation (e.g., $1.47893 \times 10^{5} = 1.5 \times 10^{5}$).

10 minutes

5. Ask students to read the directions for Exercise I (page 97) and complete it with their partners or groups. When they have finished, review the answers and discuss any problems students had in doing the exercise. Provide other examples if necessary.

15 minutes

WORKING IN SCIENTIFIC NOTATION

Numbers written in scientific notation can be added, subtracted, multiplied, and divided.

Adding and Subtracting

To add or subtract numbers in scientific notation, you must be sure that the *exponents* are the same.

You can add 4×10^3 and 3×10^3, but you cannot add 4×10^3 and 3×10^2.

If you have to add 4×10^3 and 3×10^2, you can change one of them so the exponents are the same. For example, you could say:

$$4 \times 10^3 = 4{,}000 = 40 \times 10^2$$

Then you could add 40×10^2 and 3×10^2.

Once the exponents are the same:

TO ADD: *Add the coefficients.*

$$(40 \times 10^2) + (3 \times 10^2) = (40 + 3) \times 10^2 = 43 \times 10^2 = 4.3 \times 10^3$$

TO SUBTRACT: *Subtract the coefficients.*

$$(40 \times 10^2) - (3 \times 10^2) = (40 - 3) \times 10^2 = 37 \times 10^2 = 3.7 \times 10^3$$

Multiplying and Dividing

When you multiply or divide in scientific notation, the exponents do not have to be the same.

TO MULTIPLY: *Multiply the coefficients and add the exponents.*

$$(6 \times 10^2) \times (4 \times 10^3) =$$

$$(6 \times 4) \times (10^{2 \cdot 3}) = 24 \times 10^5 = 2.4 \times 10^6$$

Multiply coefficients   Add exponents

TO DIVIDE: *Divide the coefficients and subtract the exponents.*

$$(6 \times 10^4) \div (3 \times 10^3) =$$

$$(6 \div 3) \times (10^{4 \cdot 3}) = 2 \times 10^1 = 20$$

Divide coefficients   Subtract exponents

98

6. Read "Working In Scientific Notation" (page 98) aloud, stopping as you read to work through the examples given for adding, subtracting, multiplying, and dividing in scientific notation. Provide other examples if necessary.

10 minutes

EXERCISE II

Directions: Do the problems below to practice adding, subtracting, multiplying, and dividing in scientific notation. Use the examples on page 98 for help.

1. $(6 \times 10^3) + (5 \times 10^3) =$ $\underline{(6+5) \times 10^3 = 11 \times 10^3 = 1.1 \times 10^4}$

2. $(9 \times 10^6) - (8 \times 10^6) =$ $\underline{(9-8) \times 10^6 = 1 \times 10^6}$

3. $(2 \times 10^2) \times (6 \times 10^4) =$ $\underline{(2 \times 6) \times (10^{2+4}) = 12 \times 10^6 = 1.2 \times 10^7}$

4. $(8 \times 10^8) \div (4 \times 10^3) =$ $\underline{(8 \div 4) \times (10^{8-3}) = 2 \times 10^5}$

5. $(4 \times 10^4) + (3.2 \times 10^4) =$ $\underline{(4 + 3.2) \times 10^4 = 7.2 \times 10^4}$

6. $(5.6 \times 10^5) - (3 \times 10^5) =$ $\underline{(5.6 - 3) \times 10^5 = 2.6 \times 10^5}$

7. $(3 \times 10^5) \times (9 \times 10^3) =$ $\underline{(3 \times 9) \times (10^{5+3}) = 27 \times 10^8 = 2.7 \times 10^9}$

8. $(9 \times 10^7) \div (3 \times 10^4) =$ $\underline{(9 \div 3) \times (10^{7-4}) = 3 \times 10^3}$

99

7. Have students read the directions for Exercise II (page 99) and complete it with their partners or groups. When students have finished, have a student explain how he or she solved each problem. Discuss as necessary. Provide other problems if students need more practice.

    15 minutes

130

HEATING YOUR HOME

Scientific notation can be helpful in figuring out how to keep heat in your house in the winter.

Heat is measured in British Thermal Units, or BTUs. A BTU is the amount of heat needed to raise the temperature of one pound of water one degree Fahrenheit. A gallon of fuel oil contains about 140,000 BTUs (1.4×10^5) of heat.

In the northern part of the U.S., a three bedroom house might use 1,000 (1×10^3) gallons of fuel oil each winter. To find out how many BTUs of heat this house would use, you would multiply the number of BTUs contained in one gallon of fuel oil by the total number of gallons of fuel oil used.

$$(1.4 \times 10^5) \quad \times \quad (1 \times 10^3) \quad = 1.4 \times 10^8 \text{ BTUs}$$

↑	↑
BTUs from 1 gallon of fuel oil	Total gallons of fuel oil used

This sample house uses 1.4×10^8 BTUs each winter. If you can find out how much fuel oil *your* home uses every winter, you can use the same formula to find how many BTUs you use. If your home is heated by electricity or natural gas, you can use a similar formula. One kilowatt hour contains 3,414 BTUs. One hundred cubic feet of natural gas contains 103,000 BTUs.

CONSERVING HEAT

Anything which can be done to keep heat from leaving the house saves energy and money. One way to conserve energy is to be sure that your furnace works efficiently. Other ways are:

1) insulating your house,

2) putting up storm windows to slow down the loss of heat from windows,

3) closing drapes every night and opening them in the morning, and

4) turning down the thermostat when people are out or asleep.

EXERCISE III

Directions: Work through the steps of this problem to find out how many gallons of oil can be saved by insulating the attic of a house. Use scientific notation to help work with the large numbers.

100

8. Read "Heating Your Home" (page 100) and "Conserving Heat" (page 100) aloud, or have a student read them aloud. Discuss as necessary. Note that the English unit for heat, BTU, is used rather than the comparable metric unit. This reflects common commercial usage.
5–10 minutes

9. Have students read the directions for Exercise III (page 100) and the "Background Information" (page 101) provided for this problem. Have students complete Exercise III with their partners or groups. When they have finished, discuss how much energy can be saved through insulation in this particular problem.

Students may find calculators useful in this exercise.
15 minutes

131

Background Information

Houses A and B both have 1,000 square feet of floor area in the attic. House A's attic is insulated. House B's attic is not.

House A loses .66 x 10³ BTUs every hour through the ceiling.

House B loses 3.6 x 10³ BTUs every hour through the ceiling.

1. The heating season for these houses consists of 3,000 (3 x 10³) hours.

   a) How many BTUs will House A lose through its insulated ceiling during a heating season?

   $$.66 \times 10^3 \text{ BTU/hour} \quad \times \quad 3 \times 10^3 \text{ hours} \quad = \quad \underline{1.98 \times 10^6 \text{ BTUs}}$$

          ↑   ↑   ↑

     BTUs lost each hour   **Number of hours**   **BTUs lost in a**
                                 per heating season   **heating season**

   b) How many BTUs will House B lose through its uninsulated ceiling during a heating season?

   $$3.6 \times 10^3 \text{ BTU/hour} \quad \times \quad 3 \times 10^3 \text{ hours} \quad = \quad \underline{10.8 \times 10^6 \text{ BTUs}}$$

2. How many BTUs does House A save by being insulated? Find the difference between the total number of BTUs lost in House B and House A.

   $$\underline{10.8 \times 10^6 \text{ BTUs}} \quad - \quad \underline{1.98 \times 10^6 \text{ BTUs}} \quad = \quad \underline{8.82 \times 10^6 \text{ BTUs}}$$

       ↑   ↑   ↑

     BTUs used in   **BTUs used in**   **BTUs saved**
     House B   **House A**

3. Find out how many gallons of oil are saved by insulating House A. Divide the number of BTUs saved by the number of BTUs in one gallon of oil (1.4 x 10⁵).

   $$\underline{8.82 \times 10^6 \text{ BTUs}} \quad \div \quad 1.4 \times 10^5 \text{ BTU/gallon} \quad = \quad \underline{6.3 \times 10^1 = 63 \text{ gall}}$$

       ↑   ↑   ↑

     BTUs saved   **BTUs in 1 gallon**   **Gallons saved**

101

THE COST OF SAVING ENERGY

Two of the four suggestions given on page 100 for saving energy cost no extra money. *Closing the drapes* and *turning down the thermostat* save energy and money but cost you nothing.

It does cost money to add *storm windows* or *insulation* to your house. You can find out how much it costs and compare it to how much you save. It may take several months or years to *pay back* the cost of the insulation or storm windows out of the money they save you. But once this amount of time has passed, the savings and the conservation of energy continue.

By investing money in your house to save energy, you can often save more money on heating bills than you could have earned by putting the same amount of money in the bank. You have also helped to conserve a finite source of energy.

102

10. Read "The Cost Of Saving Energy" (page 102) aloud, or have a student read it aloud. Discuss as necessary.

Additional Suggestion #2, on page 135 of the Teacher's Guide, is an exercise in which students compute the cost of insulating a house and the length of time it takes to pay back the initial expense. This exercise could be inserted at this point in the unit.

5 minutes

UNIT XII SUMMARY

SCIENTIFIC NOTATION

Scientific notation is a system for working with large numbers. In scientific notation, the number 1,000,000,000 is written as: 1.0×10^9.

The 1 is the *coefficient*.

The 9 is the *exponent*. It shows how many places the decimal point has been moved to the left.

Numbers in scientific notation can be added, subtracted, multiplied, and divided.

To ADD or SUBTRACT, the exponents must be the same.

TO ADD: Add the coefficients. Keep the exponent the same.

$$(3 \times 10^2) + (6 \times 10^2) = 9 \times 10^2$$

TO SUBTRACT: Subtract the coefficients. Keep the exponent the same.

$$(8 \times 10^4) - (4 \times 10^4) = 4 \times 10^4$$

You can multiply or divide in scientific notation even if the exponents are different.

TO MULTIPLY: Multiply the coefficients and add the exponents.

$$(2 \times 10^4) \times (6 \times 10^2) = 12 \times 10^6$$

TO DIVIDE: Divide the coefficients and subtract the exponents.

$$(9 \times 10^6) \div (3 \times 10^4) = 3 \times 10^2$$

CONSERVING ENERGY

It is not enough to trap and store solar energy for later use. We must also find ways to slow down the loss of heat from a house or building. Otherwise, much of the heat collected by the greenhouse will be wasted. Slowing down the rate of heat loss is a method of *conserving energy*.

There are many ways to conserve heat:

1) Be sure that your furnace is working efficiently.

2) Insulate the attic.

3) Put up storm windows that keep air from escaping from windows.

4) Close the drapes each night and re-open them every morning.

5) Turn down the thermostat when people are out or asleep.

All of these forms of conservation will save energy and money. The first three ways of conserving energy listed above will also cost money. It may take several months or years to *pay back* the cost of conserving out of the savings. But once the payback time has passed, the conservation and savings continue.

103

11. Review the Unit XII Summary (page 103).

Additional Suggestions for Unit XI

1. Additional practice problems for *Exercise I:*

Put each number into scientific notation:

		Write out the number shown in scientific notation:	
2,300	2.3×10^3	4.3×10^4	43,000
320	3.2×10^2	9.1×10^6	9,100,000
120,000	1.2×10^5	3.66×10^3	3,660

Additional practice exercises for *Exercise II:*

$(4 \times 10^7) + (5 \times 10^7) = \underline{\quad 9 \times 10^7 \quad\quad\quad\quad\quad\quad\quad\quad\quad\quad\quad\quad}$

$(4.2 \times 10^3) + (2 \times 10^2) = \underline{\quad (42 \times 10^2) + (2 \times 10^2) = 44 \times 10^2 = 4.4 \times 10^3}$

$(8 \times 10^2) - (4 \times 10^2) = \underline{\quad 4 \times 10^2 \quad\quad\quad\quad\quad\quad\quad\quad\quad\quad\quad\quad}$

$(6 \times 10^6) - (3 \times 10^5) = \underline{\quad (60 \times 10^5) - (3 \times 10^5) = 57 \times 10^5 = 5.7 \times 10^6}$

$(5 \times 10^3) \times (4 \times 10^6) = \underline{\quad 20 \times 10^9 = 2 \times 10^{10} \quad\quad\quad\quad\quad\quad\quad}$

$(6.1 \times 10^2) \times (3 \times 10^2) = \underline{\quad 18.3 \times 10^4 = 1.83 \times 10^5 \quad\quad\quad\quad\quad}$

$(8 \times 10^6) \div (2 \times 10^3) = \underline{\quad 4 \times 10^3 \quad\quad\quad\quad\quad\quad\quad\quad\quad\quad\quad\quad}$

$(6.3 \times 10^8) \div (3 \times 10^5) = \underline{\quad 3.3 \times 10^3 \quad\quad\quad\quad\quad\quad\quad\quad\quad\quad\quad}$

2. Have students use their answers in Exercise III to compute how much it would cost to insulate the ceiling of House A and how long it would take to pay back this cost. You should substitute the current oil prices for those given if the difference is significant, and substitute cost per KWH or Therm (100 ft^3) if electricity or natural gas is used by the majority of your students.

   Directions: Follow the steps of the problem below to find out how much it costs to insulate the ceiling of House A.

a. Suppose a gallon of oil costs about $1.25. Find out how much money House A saves by insulating the ceiling. Use your answer from Exercise III, question 4 for the number of gallons of oil saved in a heating season.

63 gallons	×	$1.25/gallon	=	$78.75
Number of gallons saved		**Cost per gallon**		**Money saved**

b. It costs about $ .30 per square foot to install insulation in an attic. How much would it cost to insulate House A, which has 1,000 (1×10^3) square feet of attic ceiling area?

$ .30/sq. ft.	×	1,000 sq. ft.	=	$300.00
Cost per square foot		**Number of square feet**		**Total cost**

c. In Step 1 you found how much money you would save each heating season by insulating your attic. In Step 2 you found how much it cost to put in the insulation. If you saved the same amount every year, how many years of saving would it take to pay back the cost of the insulation? Divide the cost of the insulation by the savings per year.

$300.00	÷	$78.75/year	=	3.8 years
Cost of insulation		**Savings per year**		**Years to pay back**

3. Have students figure out the number of BTUs delivered by an average oil burner.

> Because some heat is lost up the chimney, a furnace which is 100% efficient can still only get 80% of the BTUs in the fuel. If a home uses 1.4×10^8 BTUs in a winter, how many of those BTUs are actually available after entropy?

$$1.4 \times 10^8 \text{ BTUs} \times 80\% = 1.4 \times 10^8 \text{ BTUs} \times .8 = 1.12 \times 10^8 \text{ BTUs}$$

> Most oil burners have an efficiency of only 80%. That is, they can deliver only 80% of the energy available to them after entropy. How many BTUs would an average oil burner deliver to the home used in this example?

$$1.12 \times 10^8 \text{ BTUs} \times 80\% = 1.12 \times 10^8 \text{ BTUs} \times .8 = 8.96 \times 10^7 \text{ BTUs}$$

4. Students can begin to look at ways of conserving other forms of energy, such as electricity. They might, for example, look at the lighting used in their school, and answer some of these questions.

> *Incandescent lights use far more energy than fluorescent lights. A 150 watt incandescent light gives about the same illumination as a 40 watt fluorescent light.*

> Your classroom is probably lit with fluorescent bulbs. Count the bulbs and find out their wattage. How many watts does your classroom use?

> If the lamps were incandescent you would use four times as much. What would the wattage be if the lamps were incandescent?

> How many watts are saved by using fluorescents?

> How many hours a day are the classroom lights on?

> Multiply hours × watts × number of school days to find out the total number of watt/hours used in a school year. Divide by 1,000 to get kilowatt/hours.

> How many kilowatt hours would you save if you reduced the number of hours of usage by 1/3?

> How might you achieve this reduction?

> Find out how much your school pays per kilowatt/hour. How many dollars could be saved if every classroom in the school reduced usage by 1/3?

PART THREE:

APPROPRIATE TECHNOLOGY AT WORK

UNIT XIII: DEVELOPING AND TESTING AN HYPOTHESIS
and
APPLYING APPROPRIATE TECHNOLOGY

STUDY SKILLS

In this unit, students will work through the steps of the scientific method.

1. They OBSERVE how an appropriate technology which they design and build performs in comparison to those designed by their classmates.

2. They DEVELOP AN HYPOTHESIS about their device based on observed similarities and differences.

3. They TEST THEIR HYPOTHESIS by improving their device in a way suggested by the hypothesis and then retesting the device.

4. After observing the performance of their device a second time, they DRAW CONCLUSIONS about the accuracy of their hypothesis.

Students have practiced observing in Unit X, "Applying Scientific Laws," and have had to draw conclusions in Unit VII, "Problem Solving." This unit incorporates these skills into the scientific method and introduces the new skills of developing and testing an hypothesis.

APPROPRIATE TECHNOLOGY

Unit XIII gives students the opportunity to build devices which capture renewable energy. Through this process they discover some of the technical problems found in the application of appropriate technology. They also identify some of the variables which determine the success of such devices.

Students are given the option of building a passive solar collector, similar in function to that used in their experiments in Units IX and XI, or a wind machine. The Additional Suggestions in the Teacher's Guide for this unit include information on building an active solar collector. This can be offered to students as a third option or used as an additional activity.

NOTE: Answers have not been provided in the Teacher's Guide for this unit. Students' answers will depend on their devices and tests.

Suggested Directions for Unit XIII

1. Organize your class into groups of two to four.

2. Have students read the "Introduction" (page 104). Read "Passive Solar Collectors And Wind Machines" (pages 104–105) aloud, or have students take turns reading it aloud. Discuss the material in the data tables and the kinds of passive solar collectors and wind machines students might build.

Approximate time: 10 minutes

Wind Machine

Purpose: To make an axle turn as quickly as possible, generating energy for other uses.

Test: You will test this device by painting one blade a bright color. You will then count how many times the blade goes around in a three minute period when exposed to a wind source.

Part	Commercial Material	Your Material	Purpose
Blade(s)	light metal, wood, cloth	cardboard, balsa wood, metal, plastic, cloth	catches wind energy
Axle (may be horizontal or vertical)	metal	metal, wood, plastic	turns as blades turn, producing electrical or mechanical energy
Support tower	metal	wood, metal	supports axle and blade and raises them into wind current

WIND MACHINE

EXERCISE I

Directions: With your partner or group, build either a *passive solar collector* or a *wind machine.* The purpose and materials for each are described above. Bring your device to class. Be prepared to test it on the day set by your teacher. (Your teacher will tell you if there are size and materials limitations.)

105

3. Have students read the directions for Exercise I (page 105). You may want to have all students build the same kind of device (either passive solar collectors or wind machines). You may also want to set limits on size (e.g., less than two feet across) and materials (e.g., no aluminum foil). The goal is to allow students the flexibility to be creative while keeping the devices similar enough so that students can identify the reason(s) for differences in performance.

Tell students when the devices will be due. You may want to give students up to a week for construction. The devices can be built at home, in class, or in industrial arts class if other teachers are willing to participate in this activity. Unless you provide class time for students to work together, students must understand that it is their responsibility to meet with their partners or groups to build their devices.

Have students bring their devices to class on the assigned day.

4. Read "Scientific Method" (page 106) aloud, or have a student read it aloud. Discuss with students how this process is similar to and different from other problem solving strategies introduced in this book.

5 minutes

5. Have students read the directions for Exercise II (page 106). This exercise may be set up as a contest, so that students compete to determine which device is most successful at capturing energy. If students are testing passive solar collectors, they will need to be out in the sun or have access to a reflector lamp. Because they will need the same conditions when they re-test the device in Exercise IV, a lamp may be the best source of energy. They will also need thermometers. If they are testing wind devices, they will need a wind source. A fan will probably work best, because it will allow students to re-test their devices under the same conditions.

A note about testing wind machines: If it is a windy day or the fan is set on high, students may have difficulty counting blade rotations for three minutes. One alternative is to have them count rotations three times for a minute each time. They can then average the three numbers. Another alternative is to tie a string with a weight attached to one end to the axle of the wind machine. As the blades turn, the string will wind around the axle, pulling the weight up. Students can time how long it takes to lift the weight. If students want to compare times using this test, the weight at the end of the string and the axle diameters must be the same for each device.

Have students test their devices and compare results. You may want to make a class data table for each type of device so students can compare.

Example: **Passive Solar Collectors/Wind Machines**

NAME	TIME	CHARACTERISTICS OF DEVICE
Bob and Wendy		
Jean and Mel		
Brenda, Paul and Alice		

20–30 minutes

III. Compare your results to those of other groups

If you built a solar collector, list all of the differences you see between collectors that worked well and those that did not.

If you built a wind machine, list all of the differences between those that worked well and those that did not.

Kind of device you built: _____

Differences: _____

_____

_____

_____

_____

_____

DEVELOPING AN HYPOTHESIS

An HYPOTHESIS is an idea about why something happens the way it does. It is usually based on information that has been gathered or observed. An hypothesis is a good guess based on facts; it is not a sure thing until it has been tested and proven.

You have just gathered information about how different passive solar collectors and/or wind machines work. You can now develop an hypothesis from this information that explains what makes a passive solar collector or wind machine work most effectively. For example, one hypothesis might be:

A passive solar collector will work better if it is insulated.

EXERCISE III

Directions: Look again at the list of differences you found between devices (Exercise II, above). As a group, write three hypotheses about what makes the kind of device you built (either passive solar collector or wind machine) work most effectively.

Hypothesis 1: _____

_____

_____

Hypothesis 2: _____

_____

_____

Hypothesis 3: _____

_____

_____

107

6. Read "Developing An Hypothesis" (page 107) aloud, or have a student read it aloud. Discuss as necessary.

Have students read the directions for Exercise III (page 107) and complete it in their groups. When they have finished, have one student from each group read the group's hypothesis. Discuss.

10–15 minutes

TESTING HYPOTHESES

Once you have developed an hypothesis, you must test it to determine whether or not it is true. You can do this by changing your device in the way suggested by your hypothesis. Then, you can re-test your device to see if it is actually more effective. If it is, the hypothesis is correct. If it is not, the hypothesis is probably incorrect.

To be tested, your hypothesis should involve only one idea or part of your device. Then, you will know which one thing to change before you re-test your device and will have only one reason for any difference in its performance. For example, if your hypothesis is:

A good passive solar collector has insulation and dark-colored storage materials,

you would not know whether the change in the insulation or the change in the storage materials caused a change in performance when you re-tested your device. A better hypothesis would be:

A good passive solar collector is well insulated.

You could then change the kind or amount of insulation in your passive solar collector to test this hypothesis.

EXERCISE IV

Directions: Follow the steps below to test your hypothesis.

I. Look over the hypotheses you wrote in Exercise III (page 107). Choose one or rewrite one that you can test. Be sure that it involves changing only one thing about your device. Write the hypothesis you will test here:

_____

_____

_____

II. Change your device (improve it!) in a way that allows you to test your hypothesis.

III. Use the same test you used in Exercise II (page 106) to re-test your improved device. Remember that the conditions of the test must be the same, so that the only change is the one you made to the device. Record your results in the space provided below.

Passive solar collector: Time for temperature to fall from 21°C to 15°C:

_____

Wind machine: Number of times the blade goes around in three minutes:

_____

IV. Compare the results of your first test in Exercise II and this re-test.

Was the performance of your device improved? _____

Was your hypothesis correct? _____

108

7. Read "Testing Hypotheses" (page 108) aloud, or have a student read it aloud. Discuss as necessary.

Have students read through all of the steps of Exercise IV (page 108). You may want to have them complete this exercise one step at a time, stopping to discuss their results after each step. Have students choose one of their hypotheses to test. Give students time (in class or on their own) to improve their devices. Then, have students retest their devices, record their results, and decide whether or not their hypotheses were correct. Discuss students' results.

20–30 minutes

DRAWING A CONCLUSION

After you have observed something happening and developed and tested an hypothesis about it, you are ready to draw a *conclusion*. A conclusion is a statement which says whether or not your hypothesis is true.

For example, suppose your *hypothesis* was:

A good passive solar collector needs insulation.

If, when you added insulation to your device, you found that it was more effective at trapping and holding heat, your *conclusion* would be:

A good passive solar collector needs insulation.

If your testing proved that insulation did not result in improved performance, your *conclusion* would be:

Insulation does not improve a passive solar collector.

EXERCISE V

Directions: Write a conclusion that explains whether the hypothesis you tested in Exercise IV was true or false. Write your conclusion on the lines provided below.

CONCLUSION: _____

_____

_____

_____

8. Have students read "Drawing A Conclusion" (page 109). Discuss as necessary.

Ask students to read the directions for Exercise V (page 109) and complete it in their groups. When they have finished, have one student from each group explain the group's conclusion. *10 minutes*

UNIT XIII SUMMARY

DEVELOPING AND TESTING AN HYPOTHESIS

An hypothesis is a careful guess about why something happens. It is based on observed facts.

You can use the SCIENTIFIC METHOD to develop and test an hypothesis.

1. OBSERVE to collect information.

2. DEVELOP AN HYPOTHESIS that explains your observations.

3. TEST YOUR HYPOTHESIS through some kind of experiment, and observe your results.

4. DRAW A CONCLUSION that states whether your hypothesis was true or false.

APPROPRIATE TECHNOLOGY

Passive solar collectors and wind machines are examples of appropriate technology at work. In this unit you have seen how changes can be made to improve the performance of these technologies.

110

9. Review the Unit XIII Summary (page 110).

Additional Suggestions

1. Below is information students would need to build an active solar collector. This could be presented to students as a third option in this unit, or it could be used as a follow-up activity after the unit has been completed. Students could build active solar collectors, test them, develop hypotheses, improve and retest the collectors, and draw conclusions.

Active Solar Collector

Purpose: To heat water to the highest temperature possible.

Test: You can test an active solar collector by measuring how much the temperature of a standard quantity of water increased in a given amount of time, i.e., 1/2 liter of water increases _____°C in 20 minutes. (You will need a thermometer, containers for water, beakers to measure water, and a timing device.)

PART	COMMERCIAL MATERIAL	YOUR MATERIAL	PURPOSE
Transparent cover	glass, plexiglass	plastic wrap	allows light to enter, traps heat
Absorber plate	copper, aluminum (black on side which faces sun)	any material which absorbs heat well	absorbs heat
Pipes	copper	plastic or rubber tubing	carry heat transfer medium
Transfer medium	water, propylene glycol, air	any fluid	transports heat from absorber plate to storage
Storage medium	water, rock, air	any material which can hold heat	saves heat for use at another time
Insulation	fiberglass, styrofoam	any insulating material	keeps heat in storage tank and collector
Pump* or blower	1/4 hsp. pump or blower	aquarium pump or fan	pumps heated transfer medium from panel to storage tank

*A thermosyphoning panel needs no pump. The storage tank is placed higher than the panel and convection moves the heat transfer medium.

An active solar collector can be any size. Commercial panels are three feet by seven feet and weigh approximately 150 pounds.

UNIT XIV: PUTTING IT ALL TOGETHER

In this unit, students are asked to apply the skills and knowledge they have learned in this program to solving a school problem through the use of appropriate technology. The particular skills and ideas students use in this unit may depend on the problems they identify and choose to solve. Students should be encouraged to use other units in this book as a resource as they solve their problems.

In solving the problem, students will also be using a wide range of study skills. They will need to use problem solving methods suggested in Units VII, X, and XIII. If they choose to interview people for information, they will need to practice their listening skills. Depending on the problem they choose and the kinds of information available, students will need to read for meaning, take effective notes, and interpret charts and graphs. They may also need to use the metric system and scientific notation. Students should be encouraged to use the study skills they have learned in effectively solving their problems.

NOTES ABOUT TEACHING THIS UNIT

1. Encourage students to choose a problem which can be solved within the time limits you set for the project. Some of the examples cited on pages 112 and 113 of the student text took several years of work by teachers and students. These examples should be regarded as long-range efforts, not necessarily as direct models for your students' projects.

2. Exercises I and II can be done in one or two class periods. Exercise III asks students to carry out their project. Students will need approximately three weeks to complete a project. You will need to set a due date for the project and assign interim progress reports. You will also need to decide if students will be given class time to work on the project, and if so, how much. Communicate these decisions to students when they reach Exercise III.

3. The directions below suggest that students carry out the projects in groups of three or four. Another approach is to do a class project about a problem of concern to everyone. You will want to consider carefully which of these approaches you choose, because they offer different rewards and challenges.

UNIT XIV: PUTTING IT ALL TOGETHER

INTRODUCTION

This book has introduced you to information and ideas about appropriate technology. In this unit you will have the chance to use your knowledge in a real situation. With a group of your classmates, you will identify a problem in your school which could be solved using appropriate technology. You and your classmates will then work to solve the problem, using the science study skills and ideas you have learned in this book.

Some examples of problems worked on by other groups of students include:

1) litter,
2) wasted energy,
3) wasted food,
4) garbage disposal, and
5) transportation.

EXERCISE I

Directions: With your group, identify four problems in your school which could be solved using appropriate technology. You may want to use the list of problems above for ideas, but the problems you identify should be more specific to your situation. Write the problems on the lines provided below.

Example: In our school, lights are left on in empty classrooms so that energy is wasted.

Problems:

1. _____
   _____
   _____
   _____

2. _____
   _____
   _____
   _____

3. _____
   _____
   _____
   _____

4. _____
   _____
   _____
   _____

111

Suggested Directions for Unit XIV

1. Organize your class into groups of three or four. You may choose to assign students to groups or allow them to form their own groups. The groups will need to be able to work together on the project they choose. If you choose to do a class project, students will work in small groups on Exercise I only.

2. Have students read the "Introduction" (page 111). Discuss as necessary.

   Approximate time: 5 minutes

3. Have students read the directions for Exercise I (page 111). Emphasize that they should list problems which are specific and can be solved. They should also try to choose problems on which they can have an effect. Suggest to students that they talk to people in the school — other students, teachers, principal, custodians, secretaries, cooks — to uncover problems. You might want to invite one or more of these people into your classroom to talk to students about school problems.

   Have students complete Exercise I (page 111) in their groups. When they have finished, ask one student from each group to read the group's ideas. List each problem on the board. Discuss the problems students have identified and how they might begin to solve them.

   10–15 minutes

SOLVING THE PROBLEM

Once you have identified a problem, you have to plan a strategy for solving it. Remember how Lisa solved her problem in Unit VII?

The paragraphs below describe several examples of strategies used by students to help their communities solve problems through the use of appropriate technology. Your local problems may be different from those presented here. You may also have less time to solve your problem than some of these groups did. But perhaps their ideas will be useful to you in organizing your own problem solving project.

Examples of Local Problem Solving

1. In San Jose, California, a group of 20 third, fourth, and fifth graders formed an Energy Patrol to help their school save electricity. Each day, four Energy Patrol members picked up special jackets, name tags, and keys kept for their use in the office. During morning recess, they checked unoccupied areas to see that lights had been turned off. If the lights were on, patrol members turned them off and attached a picture of their school mascot crying about energy waste. If the lights were off, they attached a picture of the mascot smiling. The Energy Patrol saved their school thousands of kilowatt hours of electricity in each of the first three months of their project.

2. A group of Sheehan High School ninth graders in Wallingford, Connecticut were concerned about the energy being wasted in their school. They formed a group called the Wallingford Auditing Technical Team (WATT) to look at the ways their school could save energy. WATT presented its findings to the school board and convinced the board that tremendous amounts of energy could be saved through simple conservation measures like the ones you learned about in Unit XI. The board appointed WATT as its Energy Management Team. In the next two years, the school spent about $12,000 on conservation and saved over $500,000.

3. Since 1970, 250 youths in La Crescenta, California have been helping to build Sunfire, a 5-kilowatt solar collector. These students designed many parts of the collector, obtained scrap material, and did most of the construction. They plan to donate the collector to Pitcairn Island in the South Pacific. The island suffers from a severe energy shortage. The students are currently involved in developing a successful means of transporting the collector to Pitcairn Island.

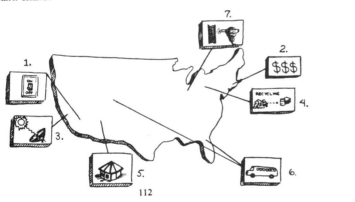

112

4. Ask students to read "Solving The Problem" (page 112). Then, read the "Examples Of Local Problem Solving" (page 112–113) aloud, or have students take turns reading them aloud. Point out that some of these projects took more than a year to complete, but they are examples of what students can do. Discuss as necessary.

Note: Examples cited were provided by:

National Commission on Resources for Youth, Inc. 605 Commonwealth Avenue Boston, MA 02215

National Energy Education Day Project P. O. Box 2518 Reston, VA 22090

Further examples can also be found through the Center for Youth Development and Research, University of Minnesota, 48 McNeal Hall, St. Paul, MN 55108

10 minutes

4. Since 1970, Riverside High School students in Ellwood, Pennsylvania have been the moving force behind an appropriate technology designed to conserve their community's energy and material resources. By 1982, these students had recycled over 2 million pounds of glass, over 1 million pounds of tin, nearly 3 million pounds of newsprint, over 50 tons of IBM cards, and about 1,000 used car batteries. As a result of their recycling efforts, Riverside students have contributed close to $6,000 toward school and community projects.

5. Navajo youth in Window Rock School District #8, Fort Defiance, Arizona demonstrated how appropriate technology could help cut their community's dependence on non-renewable energy by using a plentiful local resource, sunlight. Many of the students had been thinking of dropping out of school before the project began. Instead, they pitched in to design and build a solar hogan, an eight-sided structure which combines traditional Navajo building with modern solar technology. The hogan, which stirred interest throughout the Navajo community, may become a model for future construction projects.

6. Students in two different parts of the United States came up with very different appropriate technologies for solving transportation problems in their communities. These students were concerned about air pollution, traffic problems, and the inefficient use of energy. In Jacksonville, Florida, high school students formed Students for Mass Transit to educate citizens about the need for more public transportation. Students at George Washington High School in Denver, Colorado found another appropriate solution to a similar problem. They organized and operated a computer carpooling service which is used by many Denver businesses and state agencies.

7. Twelve teenagers in Ava, Illinois were trained to identify energy-wasting problems and how to correct them using no cost/low cost weatherization techniques. This group was a part of the Jackson County Action to Save Energy. In only 10 weeks, these students weatherized 50 homes belonging to elderly and low-income members of their community.

EXERCISE II

Directions: With your group, choose one of the problems you or your classmates have identified that you think you can help to solve. Write the problem in the space provided below.

Then, write down the information, materials, and steps you will need to take to solve the problem. Use the space provided on the next page.

PROBLEM: _____

_____

_____

113

---

5. Have students read the directions to Exercise II (page 113). Suggest to students that they choose a problem from the class list or from the four problems they identified in Exercise I. Ask students to complete Exercise II (page 113-115). Emphasize to students that the more detailed and specific they can make their responses in this exercise, the easier it will be to complete their project. You might again suggest to students that other people in the school and community may be valuable resources for them.

15 minutes

150

(Use your own paper if you need more space for any of these sections.)

Information needed to solve the problem:

Information	Where will you get it?
1. _____	_____
2. _____	_____
3. _____	_____
4. _____	_____
5. _____	_____
6. _____	_____

Materials needed to solve the problem:

Materials	Where will you get it?
1. _____	_____
2. _____	_____
3. _____	_____
4. _____	_____
5. _____	_____
6. _____	_____

Steps you will take to solve the problem:

Step	Who will do it?	By what date?
1. _____	_____	_____
_____		
_____		
2. _____	_____	_____
_____		
_____		
3. _____	_____	_____
_____		
_____		

Step	Who will do it?	By what date?
4. _____	_____	_____
_____		
_____		
5. _____	_____	_____
_____		
_____		
6. _____	_____	_____
_____		
_____		
7. _____	_____	_____
_____		

EXERCISE III

Directions: With your group, carry out your problem solving strategy. Your teacher will tell you when during the project you need to report your progress, and when the project should be completed. Present your completed project to the class in one of the ways described below.

Project presentations:

1. A written report describing your project, how you carried it out, and what your results were.

2. A feature article for the local newspaper, in which you describe your project and your results. (Read some feature stories from the paper to get an idea of the way this might be written.)

3. An oral presentation to the class which explains the problem, your planned solution, and your results. Charts and pictures will help you in this presentation.

4. A picture-presentation (for example, a bulletin board) which describes your problem, how you went about solving it, and your results. This presentation could include writing, drawings, photographs, charts, and whatever else helps to explain your project.

115

6. Have students read the directions and presentation options for Exercise III (page 115). Tell students when final presentations are due. Halfway through the project, have students turn in an interim progress report that states what steps they have completed, what problems they have encountered, and what they have left to do. Be sure to tell students when these reports are due. Students will also need to know how much (if any) class time they will have to work on the project. A schedule that shows students all of this information will help them organize and plan their project.

Example:

M	T	W	TH	F
1 Project Assigned	2	3 Class Time	4	5
8	9 Class Time	Interim 10 Report Due	11	12
15	16	17 Class Time	18	Project 19 Due

Note: Be sure to publicize students' efforts on these projects. Newspaper publicity and recognition from the mayor, school principal, the PTA, and the community will help students see the value of their efforts and maintain interest in the activity.

When students have finished their projects, have each group present what they have done to the class. Discuss what worked and what did not, and how students might be able to follow through on these or other ideas about appropriate technology in the future.

Approximately 3 weeks

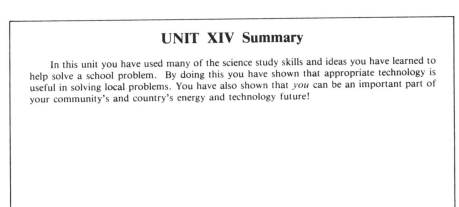

UNIT XIV Summary

In this unit you have used many of the science study skills and ideas you have learned to help solve a school problem. By doing this you have shown that appropriate technology is useful in solving local problems. You have also shown that *you* can be an important part of your community's and country's energy and technology future!

116

7. Review the Unit XIV Summary (page 116).

GLOSSARY

Acidity – The percentage of acid in something. An acid turns blue litmus paper red. Acids taste sharp and sour. Some acids may burn the skin.

Acre – A unit of area equal to 43,560 square feet.

Active solar – A technology which uses the sun's rays to produce heat and then uses electrically powered fans or pumps to move the heat where it is needed or stored for later use.

Air tight – Closed so tightly that no air or other gases can get in or out.

Anthracite – A kind of coal that is hard and makes little smoke when it burns.

Appropriate – Carefully chosen to fit the situation or use. Suitable, proper.

Atmosphere – The gas that surrounds a body in space, especially around the earth.

Back-up heating – System designed to provide heat when the main system cannot supply enough.

Barrel (of oil) – Equal to 42 gallons and to 5.6×10^6 BTU.

Billion – 1,000,000,000 or 10^9.

Biomass – Any plant material which can be turned into energy.

BTU – British Thermal Unit. One BTU can raise the temperature of one pound of water one degree Fahrenheit.

Calorie – A unit of heat in the metric system. One calorie of heat must be added to raise the temperature of one gram of water one degree Celsius.

Carbon dioxide – CO_2. A gas given off by fossil fuels when they burn in an atmosphere containing enough oxygen.

Carbon monoxide – CO. A poisonous gas given off by a fuel burning in an atmosphere containing little oxygen.

Centi- – A prefix meaning 1/100. There are 100 centimeters in a meter. One centimeter = 1/100 or .01 meter.

Climate – The average weather for a region; rainfall, temperature, winds.

Coefficient – In scientific notation, the number multiplied by the 10. In 3×10^6, 3 is the coefficient.

Commercial sector – The part of the economy consisting of offices, schools, retail stores, hospitals, nursing homes, etc.

Community – A group of people living in the same area who act together in some way.

Compost – Partially decomposed organic waste (such as leaves, food scraps, lawn clippings, animal manure) used to enrich soil.

Conduction – The transfer of heat energy from molecule to molecule within a solid. Also the transfer of heat energy from one material to another which touches it.

Conserve – Not waste, make last as long as possible.

Contract – Shrink, occupy a smaller space.

Convection – Transfer of heat energy in gases or liquids. As convection occurs, warmer matter rises and cooler matter sinks.

Converted – Changed from one form to another.

Cord (of wood) – A unit of measure for cut firewood. A cord of wood is equal to a stack that is four feet high, four feet wide, and eight feet long.

Corrode – To wear away or be worn away, especially by chemical action.

Crisis – A time of danger or difficulty in which great changes can take place.

Cubic foot – A unit of volume which is one foot by one foot by one foot.

Deposit – A pool or vein of material like oil or coal which has formed beneath the surface of the earth.

Disposal – The act of throwing away or getting rid of something.

Domestic – At home; within the country.

Efficiency – Getting good results without wasting time, materials, or effort.

Electric resistance heating – Electricity flowing through a wire heats up the wire which can be used to cook food or heat space or water.

Energy – Ability to move objects or do other kinds of physical work.

English system – A measurement system based on various common forms (foot, yard) which have now been standardized.

Entropy – A measure of the amount of energy unavailable for work, or lost through conversion.

Environment – Surroundings in which a plant or animal lives, including the air, water, and soil.

Expand – Enlarge; occupy a larger space.

Exponent – In scientific notation, the number above and to the right of the 10, indicating the number of times the decimal has been moved. It also indicates how many times 10 is to be multiplied by itself. In 3×10^6, 6 is the exponent.

Finite – Having a definite end, able to be completely used up.

First cost – The amount of money it takes to buy something.

Fluid – Matter that is able to flow; liquids and gases are fluids.

Fluorescent – A type of lighting in which gas molecules are put into motion by electric current; as a result they glow.

Fossil fuel – A burnable material formed over a period of millions of years from decaying plants and animals; oil, coal, and natural gas.

Friction – A force that slows down or stops the motion of two objects as they rub against each other.

Fuel – A material such as wood, coal, gas or oil which is burned to produce energy.

Gas – Matter in which the molecules are far apart and move so rapidly they tend to escape from an open container.

Gram – Basic unit of mass or weight in the metric system. 1,000 grams are equal to approximately 2.2 pounds in the English system.

Greenhouse effect – The increase in temperature which occurs in a closed structure when light passes through a clear material and is converted into heat.

GNP – Gross National Product. The total dollar value of all the goods and services produced in a country in a year.

Hydropower – A technology for using the energy contained in falling water to produce electricity or to perform mechanical work.

Inappropriate – Not suitable or proper for a particular situation or use.

Incandescent – A type of lighting in which a thin wire (filament) glows when electricity passes through it.

Industrial sector – The part of the economy involved in the manufacture of products and the mining of fuels and other ores.

Insulated – Surrounded with a material that slows or stops the passage of heat.

Insulation – Any material which does not conduct heat easily. Used to slow down heat loss from a house or building.

Kilo- – A prefix meaning 1,000. A kilogram = 1,000 grams; a kilowatt = 1,000 watts.

Kilowatt-hour – One thousand watts used for one hour. Ten one hundred watt light bulbs left on for an hour would use one kilowatt-hour of electricity.

Kinetic energy – Energy that has to do with motion.

Life cycle cost – The money it takes to buy, use, maintain, and eventually replace something over the entire time it is owned.

Liquid – Matter in which the molecules move more quickly than in a solid. Liquid matter takes on the shape of its container.

Liquified natural gas – To transport natural gas long distances, gas is cooled until it becomes a liquid, because it takes up less space.

Liter – Basic unit of volume in the metric system. One liter is approximately equal to one quart in the English system.

Local – Nearby.

Maintain – Keep in good working order.

Marine – Of or living in the sea.

Matter – Anything which has mass and takes up space.

Mechanical – Having to do with machines or tools.

Meter – The basic unit of length in the metric system. One meter is approximately equal to one yard in the English system.

Methane – A burnable gas which is one part of natural gas and which can also be produced from decaying organic waste.

Metric system – A system of measurement based on tens or powers of ten. In the metric system, 100 centimeters = 1 meter; 1,000 meters = 1 kilometer.

Milled – Ground up into fine pieces.

Milli- – A prefix meaning 1/1,000. A millimeter = 1/1,000 or .0001 meters.

Molecule – Two or more atoms joined by chemical bonds. A molecule is the smallest piece of matter that still has the properties of that form of matter.

Natural gas – A fossil fuel often found with petroleum.

Network – An organization which helps its members share information, goods or services with one another.

Nitrogen – An element that makes up 78% of the atmosphere.

Non-renewable – Consumed faster than it can be replaced.

Nuclear fission – The splitting of certain heavy atoms into lighter atoms. This causes the release of energy.

OPEC – Organization of Petroleum Exporting Countries.

Organic – Of or coming from living things.

Organization – A group of people who come together because they have a common interest or want to accomplish a certain task.

Passive solar – A technology which uses sunlight to heat air and water without the use of electrical fans or pumps.

Payback (or simple payback) – The time needed to save enough money to recover the cost of an investment. (Does not consider the impact of inflation.)

Petroleum – A liquid fossil fuel.

Photon – A particle of light.

Photovoltaics – A technology which turns sunlight into electricity.

Pollution – The process of making air, water, food, etc. harmful to living things; the result of this process.

Protractor – A tool used to measure angles.

Proven reserve – The portion of a coal, oil, or natural gas deposit which can be sold for more than it presently costs to get it out of the ground and prepare it for sale.

Quad – A unit of energy equal to one quadrillion BTUs.

Radiate – Send out in straight lines in all directions.

Radiation – Transfer of energy through space in all directions. Radiation can occur even in a vacuum.

Radon – A radioactive gas produced by the element radium.

Recycle – Turn into something else so that it can be used again.

Reliable – Dependable, trustworthy.

Renew – To make new or like new again; to replace.

Renewable – Capable of being renewed. A renewable resource is replaced almost as quickly as it is used.

Residential sector – The part of the economy which is made of the places in which people live, such as houses, apartments, mobile homes, condominiums, cooperatives.

Resource – A supply of something that is available for use.

Revitalized – Put new life into, brought back to life.

Rural – Having to do with the country as opposed to the city.

Scarce – Hard to find, often because there is not much left.

Scientific notation – A system for writing large numbers as single digit numbers times ten to some power. For example, $3,600,000 = 3.6 \times 10^6$.

SERI – Solar Energy Research Institute.

Shortage – Lack of enough to satisfy a need or demand.

Short ton – A unit of weight equal to 2,000 pounds.

Silicon – The second most common element found in nature, used to make photovoltaic cells.

Solar – Coming from or having to do with the sun.

Solid – Matter in which the molecules are so close together that it retains its shape.

Sprouted – Started to grow.

Standard of living – Measure of what a person spends to support his or her life; the level of comfort in everyday life.

Strip mining – Mining in an open pit after removing the earth and rock covering the deposit.

Sulfur oxides – Chemical compounds containing sulfur and water. When these combine with water they produce acids which may cause damage to buildings and may be harmful to people.

155

Sulfuric acid – Acid that results when certain sulfur oxides and water combine.

Technology – Materials and method which people use to meet their needs.

Thermal mass – Material which absorbs and stores heat.

Thermometer – A tool used to measure temperature. As the liquid in the thermometer absorbs heat, it expands. As it loses heat, it contracts.

Transportation sector – The part of the economy involved in the movement of goods and people from place to place. Includes cars, buses, trains, planes, ships, pipelines, etc.

Transported – Carried from one place to another.

Trillion – 1,000,000,000,000 or 10^{12}.

Ultimately recoverable resource – A resource which can be put to use at some future time, once it becomes profitable to mine and process it.

Uranium – A heavy element which is naturally radioactive.

Urban – Having to do with the city as opposed to the country.

Vulnerable – Unprotected from danger.

Waste – Something which is thrown away.

APPENDIX A*
Petroleum, Coal, and Natural Gas: Proven Reserves and Production

Table 1: Petroleum, Coal, and Natural Gas Proven Reserves**

RESOURCE	AS OF 1/1/80	AS OF 1/1/81	AS OF 1/1/82
Petroleum (in billion barrels)			
U.S.	29.8	29.8	29.4
World	641.6	648.5	670.3
Coal (in billion short tons)			
U.S.	472.7	Not Available	Not Available
World	975.2	Not Available	Not Available
Natural Gas (in trillion cubic feet)			
U.S.	201.0	199.0	201.7
World	2,573.2	2,638.5	2,915.0

*To update these figures, call the National Energy Information Center (DOE) at (202) 252-8800.

**U.S. (Domestic) figures from *Annual Energy Review,* 1982. World figures from *International Energy Annual* for 1979, 1980, and 1981. Both published by the Energy Information Administration, Department of Energy.

Table 2: U.S. (Domestic) Production of Petroleum, Coal and Natural Gas***

RESOURCE	1978	1979	1980	1981	1982
Petroleum					
Million barrels per day	8.71	8.55	8.60	8.57	8.67
Billion barrels per year	3.18	3.12	3.14	3.13	3.16
Coal					
Billion short tons per year	.67	.78	.83	.82	.83
Natural Gas					
Billion cubic feet	19,974.0	20,471.0	20,379.0	20,178.0	18,462.0
Trillion cubic feet	19.97	20.47	20.38	20.18	18.46

***Figures from *Monthly Energy Review,* June 1983, published by the Energy Information Administration, Department of Energy.

Table 3: Number of Years Domestic Reserves Will Last at Present Rate of Production

Petroleum

$$\frac{\text{29.4 billion barrels (Proven Reserve as of 1/1/82)}}{\text{3.16 billion barrels per year (1982 Production)}} = \text{Lasts 9.3 years}$$

Natural Gas

$$\frac{\text{201.7 trillion cubic feet (Proven Reserve as of 1/1/82)}}{\text{18.46 trillion cubic feet (1982 Production)}} = \text{Lasts 10.93 years}$$

Coal

$$\frac{\text{472.7 billion short tons (Proven Reserve as of 1/1/80)}}{\text{.83 billion short tons (1982 Production)}} = \text{Lasts 569.5 years}$$

APPENDIX B

Units of Energy

BTU Values of Energy Sources (approximate)

Coal (per 2,000 pound ton)

Anthracite	25.4×10^6 BTU
Bituminous	26.2×10^6 BTU
Sub-bituminous	19.0×10^6 BTU
Lignite	13.4×10^6 BTU

Natural Gas (per cubic foot)

Dry	1,031 BTU
Wet	1,103 BTU
Liquid (average)	4,100 BTU

1 Therm = 100 cubic feet of natural gas
1 Therm = 103,000 BTU

Electricity

1 kilowatt-hour (at home)	3,413 BTU
1 kilowatt-hour (at the power plant)	11,600 BTU

Petroleum (per 42 gallon barrel)

Crude Oil	5.60×10^6 BTU
Residual Fuel Oil	6.29×10^6 BTU
Distillate Fuel Oil	5.83×10^6 BTU
Gasoline (inc. aviation gas)	5.25×10^6 BTU
Jet Fuel (kerosene)	5.67×10^6 BTU
Jet Fuel (naphtha)	5.36×10^6 BTU
Kerosene	5.67×10^6 BTU

Nuclear

1 gram (0.0353 oz.) of fissioned
Uranium 235 = 74,000,000 BTU

1 kilowatt-hour electricity equals
0.88 pounds coal
0.076 gallons oil
10.4 cubic feet natural gas

1 tcf (trillion cubic feet or 10^{12}) natural gas equals
39.3×10^6 tons coal
184.0×10^6 barrels oil

1 million tons of coal equals
4.48×10^6 barrels of oil
6.7×10^1 tons of oil
25.0×10^{12} cubic feet natural gas

1 million tons of oil equals
6.65×10^6 bbl. oil
4.0×10^9 kwh electricity (when used to generate power)
1.5×10^6 tons of coal
41.2×10^9 cubic feet natural gas

BIBLIOGRAPHY
Energy and Appropriate Technology

Abelson, Philip H. *Energy: Use, Conservation, and Supply*. Washington, D.C.: American Association for the Advancement of Science, 1974.

Technical articles dealing with fossil fuels and alternative energy sources.

Annual Review of Energy. Palo Alto, CA: Annual Reviews, Inc.

(4139 El Camino Way, Palo Alto, CA 94306)

Boston Urban Gardeners, Statler Office Building, Room 831, 20 Park Plaza, Boston, MA 02116.

Campbell, Stu. *Let It Rot!* New York: Garden Way Publishing, 1975.

The home gardener's guide to composting.

The Cornucopia Project Newsletter. Emmaus, PA: Rodale Press. A project of the Regenerative Agriculture Association. Published quarterly.

Darrow, Ken and Pam, Rick. *Appropriate Technology Sourcebook*, Volumes I and II. Stanford, CA: Appropriate Technology Project, Volunteers in Asia, 1981.

A guide to practical books and plans for village and small community technology. Access to tools and technologies that use local skills, local resources, and renewable sources of energy. (Appropriate Technology Project, Box 4543, Stanford, CA 94305)

DeMoll, Lane and Lee, Gigi, eds. *Stepping Stones: Appropriate Technology & Beyond*. New York: Schocken Books, 1978.

Collection of essays by E. F. Schumacher, Tom Bender, Ivan Illich, Wendell Barry, etc., which comprise the philosophical stepping stones that have helped shape the techniques, tools and politics of appropriate technology.

Energy and Education Newsletter. Washington, D.C.: National Science Teachers Association. Quarterly.

Good source of information useful in the classroom about fuels, activities, films, books, conferences. (NSTA, 1742 Connecticut Avenue, NW, Washington, D.C. 20009)

Energy and Power. San Francisco: W. H. Freeman and Co., 1971.

Eleven articles from September 1971 issue of *Scientific American* which present a detailed discussion of energy and power.

"Energy: Facing Up to the Problem, Getting Down to Solutions." *National Geographic Magazine,* February 1981.

Balanced summary of fossil fuels and major renewable energy sources available in the world. Infrared photographs show heat loss from homes.

Environment. New York, NY: Scientists Institute for Public Information. Published monthly.

Environment and Energy: A Report of the United Nations Economic Commission for Europe. Elmsford, NY: Pergamon Press, 1979.

Environmental aspects of energy production and use with particular reference to new technologies.

Environmental Trends. Washington, D.C.: Council on Environmental Quality, 1981.

Graphs documenting trends in energy, transportation, material use, solid waste, toxic substances, wildlife, water quality, and more.

Fowler, John M. *Energy-Environment Source Book,* Volumes I and II. Washington, D.C.: National Science Teachers Association, 1980.

Volume I: Energy, Society, and the Environment. Volume II: Energy: Its Extraction and Use.

Fowler, John M. *Energy Factsheets*. Washington, D.C.: National Science Teachers Association.

Easy to understand descriptions of many new technologies.

Hayes, Denis. *Worldwatch Paper 4: Energy: The Case for Conservation*. Washington, D.C.: Worldwatch Institute, 1976.

Demonstrates that the cheapest potential source of energy available to the U.S. today is that which can be obtained by conservation, which also lessens the environmental threats posed by new technologies. (Worldwatch Institute, 1776 Massachusetts Ave., NW, Washington, D.C. 20036)

International Energy Annual. Washington, D.C.: Energy Information Administration, Department of Energy.

Statistics on energy supply and consumption.

Jequier, Nicolas. *Appropriate Technology: Problems and Promises.* Part I: The Major Policy Issues. Stanford, California: Appropriate Technology Project, Volunteers in Asia, 1977.

Overview of appropriate technology movement. Includes historical examples of nations which developed technologies that closely fit their needs, obstacles to implementation of appropriate technology. (Appropriate Technology Project, Box 4543, Stanford, CA 94305)

Lovins, Amory. "Energy Strategy: The Road Not Taken." *Foreign Affairs,* October 1976.

Compares economics of centralized versus decentralized energy systems; two scenarios of the future.

Melcher, Joan. *Connections.* Butte, Montana: National Center for Appropriate Technology, 1980.

A curriculum in appropriate technology for fifth and sixth graders.

Mollison, Bill and Holmgren, David. *Permaculture One: A Perennial Agriculture for Human Settlements.* Winters, CA: International Tree Crops Institute, 1981.

Unique strategies for creating a food producing system specifically suited to your needs.

Monthly Review of Energy. Washington, D.C.: Energy Information Administration, Department of Energy.

Statistics on energy supply and consumption.

New England Energy Situation and Alternatives for 1985. Boston, MA: Department of Energy Region I.

Good source of charts on energy use in New England, United States, and world. Similar publications should be available from other regional offices.

A New Prosperity: Building A Sustainable Energy Future: Andover, MA: Brick House Publishing, 1981.

Exhaustive study of potential of solar energy and conservation to achieve energy independence for the United States by the year 2000.

Packard, Vance. *The Waste Makers.* New York: D. McKay Co., 1960.

Exposes and condemns planned obsolescence and throw-away society.

Patterns of Energy Consumption in the United States. Washington, D.C.: Office of Science and Technology, Executive Office of the President, 1972.

Quammen, David. *Appropriate Jobs, Common Goals of Labor, and Appropriate Technology.* NCAT Brief 3. Butte, MT: National Center for Appropriate Technology, 1980.

Examines relationships among energy, employment opportunity, and appropriate technology. Demonstrates potential of appropriate technology to foster full, more humane employment.

Rainbook, Resources for Appropriate Technology. New York: Schocken Books, 1977.

Guide to the information, places, and people who offer and are making appropriate devices in the fields of communication, transportation, shelter, agriculture, health, waste recycling, and energy.

Ris, Thomas F., ed. *Energy and Man's Environment.* Seattle, WA: Energy and Man's Environment, 1973.

Elementary through secondary interdisciplinary activity guide. (Energy and Man's Environment, 2121 Fifth Avenue, Seattle, WA 98121)

Schumacher, E. F. *Small Is Beautiful, Economics As If People Mattered.* New York: Harper and Row, 1973.

Eloquent expression of the precepts upon which appropriate technology is based, by the movement's founder.

Science Magazine. Washington, D.C.: American Association for the Advancement of Science. Published weekly.

Scientific American. New York, NY. Published monthly.

Securing America's Energy Future: The National Energy Policy Plan. Washington, D.C.: U.S. Department of Energy, 1981.

A report to Congress which defines the Reagan Administration approach for reformulation of policy. Presents the nation's energy outlook as of 1981.

Solar Program Assessment: Environmental Factors. Washington, D.C.: Assessments Branch, Division of Solar Energy, Energy Research and Development Administration, 1977.

Assesses environmental impact of solar energy technologies, including air and water quality, land use, etc.

Stobaugh, Robert and Yergin, Daniel. *Energy Future.* New York: Random House, 1979.

Report of the energy project at the Harvard Business School. Stresses choice of conservation and solar energy over all other technologies.

Sun Times. Washington, D.C.: Solar Lobby. Monthly newsletter.
(Solar Lobby, 1001 Connecticut Ave., NW, Washington, D.C. 20036)

Wearne, Robert A., ed. Community Gardening: A A Handbook. Brooklyn, NY: Brooklyn Botanical Garden Record, Plants and Gardens, Vol. 35(1), May 1979.
Getting started, rewards and pitfalls, public and private organizations, on-site experiences across the country.

World Energy Outlook. Washington, D.C.: International Energy Agency, Organization for Economic Cooperation and Development, 1982.

More than 180 statistical tables and full texts of energy policy guidelines adopted by the International Energy Agency. Forecasts for world energy to the year 2000. (OECD Publications & Information Center, 1750 Pennsylvania Ave., NW, Suite 1207, Washington, D.C. 20006)

Solar Energy and the Greenhouse

Aaboe, Erik and Matthaie, Amy. Building Your Solar Greenhouse: A Do It Yourself Construction Guide. Santa Fe, NM: The New Mexico Solar Energy Association, 1980.

(The New Mexico Solar Energy Association, P.O. Box 2004, Santa Fe, NM 87501)

Anderson, Bruce and Wells, Malcolm. Passive Solar Energy: The Homeowner's Guide to Natural Heating and Cooling. Andover, MA: Brick House Publishing, 1981.

Carter, Joe, ed. Solarizing Your Present Home: Practical Solar Heating Systems You Can Build. Emmaus, PA: Rodale Press, 1981.

Gardening for All Seasons: The Complete Guide to Producing Food at Home, 12 Months a Year. Andover, MA: Brick House Publishing Company, 1983.

Mazria, Edward. The Passive Solar Energy Book. Emmaus, Pennsylvania: Rodale Press, 1979.

McCullagh, James C., ed. The Solar Greenhouse Book. Emmaus, PA: Rodale Press, 1978.

Northeast Sun. Brattleboro, VT: New England and Mid-Atlantic Solar Energy Associations. Published bimonthly.

Solar Age Magazine. Harrisville, NH: Solar Vision, Inc.

Wolf, Ray, ed. Solar Growing Frame. Emmaus, PA: Rodale Press, 1981.

Yanda, Bill and Fisher, Rick. The Food and Heat-Producing Solar Greenhouse: Design, Construction and Operation. Santa Fe, NM: John Muir Publications, Inc., 1976, 1980.